AUTHORS: CRITICAL AND BIOGRAPHICAL REFERENCES

A guide to 4,700 critical and biographical passages in books

by

RICHARD E. COMBS

The Scarecrow Press, Inc.
Metuchen, N.J.   1971

"The Library of Congress Cataloged the Original Printing of
This Title as:".

Combs, Richard E
    Authors: critical and biographical references; a guide to
4,700 critical and biographical passages in books, by
Richard E. Combs. Metuchen, N. J., Scarecrow Press, 1971.

    221 p.   22 cm.

    1. Literature—History and criticism—Indexes. 2. Authors—Biog-
raphy—Indexes.   I. Title.

PN524.C58   016.809   73-167644
ISBN 0-8108-0448-4   MARC

Library of Congress   71 ₍60-2₎

for Adele

Table of Contents

	Page
Introduction	vii
Directions for use	viii
Author citations	11
Key to symbols	155
Author index to books analyzed	199

v

INTRODUCTION

Authors: critical and biographical references is an analysis of nearly 500 books containing literary criticism written in English. ACBR grew out of a need to extend bibliographic control into those critical works whose contents are not apt to be reflected in a card catalog. It is intended to serve as a guide to those searching for information on any writer, regardless of his time or language.

In this work of some 4,700 references, well over 1,400 authors are noted. Each of the references cited is at least six pages in length, and most are considerably longer. The mere mention of an author has not been enough to signal inclusion; instead those pages were sought where substantive remarks begin. For purposes of this book, an "author" is any writer about whom some critical or biographical material has been written.

Most of the references are, of course, critical in nature, but many are partly or wholly biographical, and these are indicated. ACBR is intended for no specialized audience; the works it analyzes are as usable by the university student or faculty member as by the youngest scholar.

Critical works dealing entirely with one author have been excluded, as have most encyclopedic works.

As in any work of this kind, a number of people have contributed in various ways. Thanks are due Freda Thorson, Marjorie Christmann, Charlyn Costello, Mary Arends, Iona Combs, Barbara Fitzgerald, Ann Haines, Terry Hallen and Karen Wolf. My special gratitude goes to Marguerite Smith, whose work in preparing the manuscript went well beyond that of typing from one format into another. Her judgment, here as elsewhere, has proved invaluable. As for my wife Adele, she has given generously of her patience, her time and her humor, all necessary ingredients in the accomplishment of this book.

Evanston, Illinois

DIRECTIONS FOR USE

Part I. Author citations

      This section lists each author noted. Beneath each author is to be found; 1) the symbols representing the book or books in which references to that author are found, and, 2) the pagination for those references. For example:

      Jeffers, Robinson

AMPP	469-477
BPSW	204-212(b)
HIAP	398-410
INTE	109-115
MOAM	183-203
POOT	18- 24
POPO	129-134

      Of these seven citations, the second contains biographical material on Robinson Jeffers, as indicated by the "(b)" following the pagination. The user must turn to the "Key to symbols" section to learn which titles are represented by the symbols AMPP, BPSW, etc.

Part II. Key to symbols

      Here those books analyzed are listed alphabetically by symbol. This section also gives relatively full bibliographic detail, such as: author, title, place of publication, publisher and date. For example:

AMPP   Waggoner, Hyatt H.
               American poets from the Puritans to the present.
               Boston, Houghton, 1968.

BPSW   Powell, Lawrence Clark
Bookman's progress.
Los Angeles, Ward Ritchie Press, 1967.

Part III.   Author index to books analyzed

     An author arrangement of those works analyzed, giv-
ing brief title information and listing the symbols for each
title. As:

Abel, Lionel, Metatheatre.   META

Adereth, M., Commitment in modern French.   COMF

Albert, Edward, A history of English literature.   HIEL

Alexandrova, Vera, A history of Soviet literature.   HISL

Allen, Everett S., Famous American humorous poets. FAAH

Alter, Robert, After the tradition.   AFTR

AUTHOR CITATIONS

Abbott, George		Adams, Franklin Pierce	
AMDR	151-158	FAAH	9- 17

Abel, Lionel		Adams, Henry	
AGIN	133-139	CYAL	191-200
		DROR	233-248
Abélard, Peter		EVHO	204-215
CLGR	29- 36	FERE	193-205
Abell, Kjeld		INDR	374-430
GESC	466-475	LIOA	782-789
		MACA	214-227 v. 3
Abramowich, Shalom Yá Akov see Mendelé Mokher Sefarim		POSU	271-289

Adamov, Arthur		Adams, John	
DIPA	223-228	LIHA	93- 99
THAB	47- 78	MACA	307-320 v. 1
THPP	26- 36	Adams, Samuel	
Adams, Brooks		LIHAR	1- 17
MACA	227-236 v. 3	MACA	233-247 v. 1

Addams, Jane

BOTC   165-174

Addison, Joseph

COES   85- 94

CORE   137- 51 v.1

GRCR   432-440

HICR   437-448

LERB   408-474

LIHE   870-881

LIHIB   870-881

LISH   254-260

SELE   154-168

Ade, George

BIBM   101-106

RIFA   190-197

Aeschylus

ANCR   177-182

DETR   187-193

GRWA   239-257

HIGL   241-267

HIGR   79- 84

LAGL   124-136

MADR   17- 39

SPTR   61- 77

Agee, James

NOVA   212-230

Agnon, Shmuel Yosef

AFTR   131-150

FISL   48- 53

MATM   177-232

Aiken, Conrad

AMPP   477-486

BABY   85- 93

HIAP   217-225

LIBN   7- 12

MOMP   63- 74

WOWE   254-263

Aksakov, Sergei

LINL   413-419

Alain

FRPC   96-121

Albee, Edward

AMPL   81- 98

MOAP   273-286

OCLI	225-231	Alger, Horatio	
THPP	275-284	MAWH	76- 88
WWTS	321-346		
		Algren, Nelson	
Alcaeus		AMMO	187-194
HIGL	130-138	FIFO	73- 85
		WWFS	231-249
Alcott, Amos Bronson			
FLNE	240-245	Allen, James Lane	
FLNE	280-286	AMFH	472-483
		CAAN	186-191
Aldrich, Thomas Bailey			
AMFH	214-220	Allston, Washington	
DEAS	211-216	FLNE	165-170
MACA	54- 60 v. 3		
		Altizer, Thomas J.	
RIAN	579-591		
		COPT	85- 90
Aldridge, John W.			
		Ames, Fisher	
MAMF	45- 66		
		MACA	279-288 v. 2
Aleichem, Sholom			
		Amis, Kingsley	
CONT	271-278		
		BIBM	274-281
MATM	16- 24		
		POBF	34- 50
YILI	61- 98		
		Ammons, A. R.	
Alfieri, Vittorio			
		ALWA	1- 17
HIIL	365-375		

13

Anderson, Maxwell

   AMDR   288-305

   HIAD   266-271 v. 2

   MADR   678-683

   MOAP   118-134

   READ   75- 89

   SHLI   674-680

Anderson, Sherwood

   AFGT   74- 82

   AMNF   154-165

   CAAN   311-318

   COYE   520-527

   FIMA   3- 22

   LAPR   223-284

   MAWH   166-177

   WOWE   306-316

   WOWE   324-330

Andreas-Salomé, Lou

   MOWO   88- 95

Andreev, Lionid Nikolaivich

   ESRN   262-277

   GRBR   346-363

Anouilh, Jean

   DIPA   110-124

   MOFT   112-130

Antoninus, Brother

   COAP   84-100

Apollinaire, Guillaume

   CLGR   88- 93

Apollonius

   HIGL   728-736

Apuleius, Lucius

   HILL   339-350

   IDAE   12- 19

Aquinas, Saint Thomas see
   Thomas Aquinas, Saint

Aragon, Louis

   COMF   81-125

   COMF   196-207

Arden, John

   ANTH   72- 86

   MOBD   83-116

   THPP   267-273

Arendt, Hannah

    WROW   54- 71

Ariosto, Lodovico

    HIIL   185-195

Aristophanes

    ELCO   xi-xxi

    GRWA   126-158

    HIGL   425-449

    HIGR   100-109

    LAGL   194-208

    MADR   79- 91

    TILI   72- 82

Aristotle

    ANCR   236-244

    ARIS   v-xxvi

    BAWA   xi-xxxiv

    CRAL   23- 49

    ECGR   94-103

    HICL   29- 59

    HIGL   547-576

    HIGR   147-156

    INAR   ix-xxix

    LISH   21- 52

    NIET   ix-xxiv

    ONMU   xi-xliii

    POAR   vii-xvi

    POLI   5- 27

    PRTR   21- 47

    RHGR   41- 50

Armour, Richard Willard

    FAAH   18- 24

Arnold, Matthew

    BRVL   133-144

    BRVL   435-456

    CRAL   377-388

    ESFD   72- 77

    HICT   515-537

    HIOM   155-180

    IMSC   88- 98

    LIHE   1407-1415

    LIHIC   1407-1415

    LISH   436-451

    RIFM   45- 61

    VIDE   220-227

    VILI   103-120

    WIHO   366-371

Artaud, Antonin

    AMLA   94-107

    DIPA   203-209

    MOFT   224-233

    NELI   35- 49

    THPP   13- 27

Artsybashev, Mikhail
  Petrovich

    ESRN   248-261

Arvin, Newton

    BIBM   555-560

Asch, Sholem

    YILI   221-261

Ashbery, John

    ALWA   18- 37

Asimov, Isaac

    SETO   249-265

Asturias, Miguel Angel

    INMA   68-101

Atherton, Gertrude

    CACL   103-114(b)

Attaway, William

    NASO   47- 64

    NENO   132-140

Auchincloss, Louis

    AFTE   3- 9

Auden, W. H.

    BIBM   355-363

    IMSC   249-254

    INDI   143-169

    LILC   18- 26

    MOMP   120-136

    MOPE   359-394

    MOPO   165-182

    MOPR   182-202

    MOWO   19- 29

    PLDO   301-315

    POOT   378-392

    POPO   167-173

Audiberti, Jacques

    THPP   73- 84

Augustine, Saint (Aurelius
  Augustinus)

    HILL   438-443

Austen, Jane

AGFI	27- 62
ARFI	55- 78
ARNO	93-101
BEJA	332-386
BEYC	31- 56
CAEN	142-151
CHEL	117-124
CLCO	196-203
COES	144-154
CORE	191-206 v.1
ENNO	99-111
ENNO	346-360
INEN	90-104
LIHE	1200-1206
LIHIC	1200-1206
MIRO	17- 41
NOFI	115-146
NOVE	95-110
OPSE	206-230
POSU	129-150
REND	97-112
SELE	175-186
WOEL	153-178
WOVN	48- 57
WOWE	61- 79

Austin, Mary

CAAN	230-235
CACL	44- 51(b)
COYE	346-351

Babel, Isaac

BEYC	119-144
BREA	312-331
HISL	124-134
SORL	67- 72

Bachmann, Ingeborg

GEML	187-212

Bage, Robert

BEJA	273-291

Bagehot, Walter

HIOM	180-185
RIFM	75- 81
VILI	37- 52

Baldwin, James

BLAW	169-215

Baldwin, James (cont.)

    BLAWP   171-186

    COAN   155-169

    CRPR   7- 18

    ETAN   209-216

    KICA   208-214

    NASO   102-126

    NENO   215-239

    STAN   22- 27

Balzac, Honoré de

    ARFI   109-133

    FAOR   81-125

    FRLI   195-211

    LICR   469-482

    LINL   327-340

    MIRO   83- 96

    TILI   337-343

    WITS   171-182

Bancroft, George

    FLNE   130-138

    LIOA   520-525

Barker, James Nelson

    HIAM   136-151

Barlow, Joel

    AMPP   24- 30

    MACA   382-389 v. 1

Barnes, Djuna

    CLGR   139-146

    LASA   240-253

Barrie, J. M.

    ENLT   28- 35

    LILC   32- 41

Barry, Philip

    AMDR   163-180

    HIAD   275-282 v. 2

    MOAP   78- 98

    READ   196-201

Barth, John

    FABU   135-173

    OCLI   238-243

    TRWO   220-226

Barth, Karl

    COPT   97-106

Barthes, Roland

    NELI   185-194

Barthelme, Donald

    CONR   42- 52

Bartram, William

    WOWI   84- 90

Bassani, Giorgio

    COEN   156-161

Bataille, Georges

    NELI   91-102

Baudelaire, Charles Pierre

    CLGR   73- 79

    CLRE   238-243

    FRLI   285-292

    HIOM   434-452

    ILLU   157-196

    LIOS   8- 88

    OPRI   151-161

    ROAG   40- 45

    STHT   263-279

Baum, L. Frank

MASM   255-267

Baxter, Richard

    POMI   66- 72

Beard, Charles A.

    BOTC   185-196

Beaumont, William

    BOTC   36- 46

Beauvoir, Simone de

    FRPC   325-343

Beckett, Samuel

    CONE   19- 39

    CONTI   167-175

    DIPA   210-217

    FLJB   67-107

    FONN   111-125

    FOPP   87-131

    IOGE   224-231

    LINL   315-320

    LISI   120-200

    META   134-140

    MOBD   58- 65

    MOFT   193-220

Beckett, Samuel (cont.)

MORL	48- 55
NEFN	47- 54
NELI	75- 90
OCLI	255-285
PRTR	244-265
STCL	128-135
STCL	138-155
THAB	1- 46
THPP	37- 51

Beckford, William

BEJA	233-242

Bécquer, Gustavo Adolfo

LAPO	125-156

Beerbohm, Max

AMLI	176-198
BIBM	41- 62
CLCO	431-441
KICA	29- 34
LILC	53- 58

Béguin, Albert

CRCO	49- 73

Behan, Brendan

ANTH	102-108
CONT	240-246

Behrman, S. N.

AMDR	180-205
AMPL	130-136
READ	203-211

Belasco, David

HIAD	163-199 v.1

Belinsky, Vissarion

HIOC	243-264

Belitt, Ben

POOP	48- 57

Bell, Horace

CACL	279-290(b)

Bellamy, Edward

BOTC	100-109
MACA	302-315 v.3

Belloc, Hilaire

LILC	60- 65

Bellow, Saul

AFTR	95-115
AMMO	210-224
COAN	80- 94
CONT	217-223
CONTI	222-227
CRPR	112-130
ETAN	216-223
FIFO	241-262
LANI	35- 54
LASS	392-397
LUGO	127-180
MAIT	159-166
MYPO	218-224
NENA	29-107
OCLI	286-299
ORUN	194-203
RAIS	290-324
REAM	7- 18
REHV	94-102
REHV	299-305
STCL	103-116
STCL	138-155
WWTS	175-196

Bely, Andrei

RUNO	325-345

Benda, Julien

OBCO	187-200

Benét, Stephen Vincent

HIAP	431-438

Benn, Gottfried

COSG	324-364

Bennett, Arnold

AMBL	212-220
ARNO	238-243
CAEN	441-457
ENLT	185-198
LILC	65- 77
LINL	169-175
REND	303-319
RIFM	211-218

Benson, Stella

LILC	78- 83

Bentley, E. C.

MUFP	113-119

21

Benton, Thomas Hart

  VILA   23- 36

Berceo, Gonzalo de

  LAPO   3- 24

Berdichevsky, Mikhah Yosef

  MATM   124-144

Berdyaev, Nicholas

  COPT   134-149

Berenson, Bernard

  COYE   443-448

Bergelson, Dovid

  YILI   426-448

Bergson, Henri

  FRPC   30- 46

Berkeley, Anthony

  MUFP   144-149

Berkovitz, Itzhak Dov

  MATM   148-165

Bernard of Clairvaux, Saint

  CLGR   22- 29

Berryman, John

  MODP   111-124

  OCLI   526-531

  POOP   94-103

Betti, Ugo

  UGBE   vii-xviii

Bierce, Ambrose

  AMEI   166-173

  COYE   196-210

  PAGO   617-634

  RIFA   162-178

Bird, Robert Montgomery

  HIAM   220-248

  LIOA   473-482

  RIAN   246-258

Bishop, Elizabeth

  AMPO   67- 79

  COAP   72- 83

  PLDO   331-338

Bishop, John Peale

  BIBM   6- 15

  ESFD   348-357

Blake, William

    LIHE   1128-1135

    LIHIC   1128-1135

    LIRE   35- 47

    PRTR   172-179

Blanchot, Maurice

    CRCO   221-265

    NEFN   61- 66

Bloch, Robert

    SETO   335-351

Bloomgarden, Solomon see
    Yehoash

Blunden, Edmund

    LILC   92- 99

Bly, Robert

    ALWA   38- 48

Boccaccio, Giovanni

    ENEI   192-200

    HIIL   101-112

    HICL   457-464

    MAEN   134-155

    TILI   154-161

Boileau-Despréaux, Nicolas

    HICR   280-300

Boker, George Henry

    HIAM   337-364

    LIOA   487-497

Böll, Heinrich

    COEN   79- 89

    GEML   141-158

    SHGO   185-205

Bonhoeffer, Dietrich

    COPT   21- 50

Bontempelli, Massimo

    MOIN   186-196

Borel, Pétrus

    ROAG   131-137

Borges, Jorge Luis

    DREA   9- 17

    ELFI   83- 88

    INMA   102-136

Borgese, Guiseppe Antonio

    MOIN   225-233

Boucher, Jonathan		Boyd, Ernest	
LIHA	317-328	EXRE	190-195
Boucicault, Dion		Brackenridge, Hugh Henry	
HIAM	368-388	LIHAR	210-224
		LIHAR	297-302
Bourjaily, Vance		MACA	390-395 v.1
AFTE	177-191	RIAN	43- 60
Bousquet, Joë		Bradbury, Ray	
FONN	95-109	SETO	352-373
Bowen, Elizabeth		Brandes, Georg	
CONE	107-130	HIOM	356-369
LILC	108-116		
LUGD	17- 55	Brecht, Bertolt	
VAHE	146-169	COTH	218-242
		FOPP	3- 45
Bowen, John		ILLU	149-156
POBF	114-127	LIFD	136-142
		META	86-107
Bowers, Edgar		SEPB	xiii-li
ALWA	49- 56		
Bowles, Paul		Brenner, Yosef Haiyim	
FIFO	283-288	MATM	80-100
REHV	254-260		

Breton, André

MICF 145-151

Brewer, William H.

CACL 115-127(b)

Brieux, Eugène

BLES i-xxxvi

Brinnin, John

POOP 72- 93

Broch, Hermann

DIMN 138-180

Brod, Max

ILLU 141-148

Bromfield, Louis

CLCO 153-160

Brontë, Charlotte

AGFI 91-103

BRVL 281-298

CAEN 304-318

COES 185-190

CORE 219-225 v.1

LIHE 1370-1376

LIHIC 1370-1376

REND 169-183

VIDE 159-135

VINO 100-135

WOVN 153-169

WOWE 80- 96

Brontë, Emily

AGFI 77- 91

ARFI 215-243

BRVL 281-298

CAEN 304-318

CHEL 124-134

ENNO 153-170

ENNO 390-401

INEN 139-155

NOFI 91-114

NOVE 173-190

REIM 130-146

REND 184-196

VIDE 159-170

VINO 136-182

WOVN 225-245

Brooke, Rupert

ENLT 305-311

Brooke, Rupert (cont.)

    HERT   36- 45

Brooks, Cleanth

    LASA   485-501

Brooks, Gwendolyn

    BLAWP   89- 98

Brooks, Van Wyck

    AFGT   57- 68

    BIBM   107-113

    CLCO   10- 18

    CLCO   224-230

    MAWH   213-228

Brown, Charles Brockden

    AMFH   25- 49

    LODA   73- 80

    LODA   129-148

    MIAN   2- 9

    RIAN   69-104

Brown, Norman O.

    AGIN   256-262

    AMLI   114-131

Brown, William Hill

    LODA   96-105

Browning, Elizabeth Barrett

    COES   209-218

    CORE   218-231 v. 2

Browning, Robert

    BRVL   71-102

    HIEL   375-381

    LIHE   1392-1404

    LIHIC   1392-1404

    POPO   308-314

    VIDE   196-206

    VILI   78-102

    WIHO   316-332

Brunetière, Ferdinand

    HIOM   58- 71

Brunner, Emil

    COPT   106-112

Bruno, Giordano

   HIIL   282-288

Bryant, William Cullen

   AMPP   34- 42

   AMSL   101-106

   BEDA   28- 39

   COOC   165-174

   LIOA   248-261

   MACA   238-246 v. 2

   ROAL   86- 92

   SHRE   136-145

   WOWI   195-204

Buber, Martin

   COPT   117-133

Büchner, Georg

   COSG   170-200

   DETR   270-281

   ORUN   160-167

Buechner, Frederick

   RAIS   153-161

Bulwer-Lytton, Edward

   CAEN   173-180

   FAOR   285-296

Bunyan, John

   CAEN   23- 30

   CHEL   101-108

   ENEI   386-406

   ENNO   21- 32

   ENNO   288-295

   LIHE   797-802

   LIHIB   797-802

   SELE   146-153

Buonarroti, Michelangelo

   COPS   xi-xxvi

   COPS   xxvii-lvi(b)

   COPS   189-317(b)

Burgess, Anthony

   AFTE   29- 47

   OCLI   300-305

   REHV   269-275

Burke, Edmund

   LIHE   1089-1094

   LIHIB   1089-1094

   MOWO   161-167

Burke, Kenneth

    ORUN   210-220

Burney, Frances

    BEJA   204-225

Burns, Robert

    GRCR   641-646

    HIEL   245-251

    LIHE   1102-1108

    LIHIB   1102-1108

    POPO   68- 81

    WIHO   217-227

Burroughs, Edgar Rice

    EXIN   172-188

Burroughs, John

    TIMW   440-453

Burroughs, William

    AMLI   367-381

    REHV   247-253

    STCL   88- 94

    WAFE   163-169

    WROW   42- 53

    WWTS   141-174

Butler, Samuel

    AGFI   327-333

    CAEN   416-422

    DAEC   226-233

    INENO   35- 48

    LIHE   733-738

    LIHIB   733-738

    LINL   140-147

    SHLI   557-565

    VIDE   315-320

    WOVN   425-449

    WRWC   11- 25

Butor, Michel

    NEFN   69- 77

Butti, Enrico Annibale

    MOIN   119-124

Byrd, William

    COOC   27- 32

Byron, George Gordon

    AMLA   26- 42

    DETR   201-214

    HIEL   307-314

LICR	551-573	Cable, George Washington	
LIHE	1219-1229	AMFH	345-351
LIHIC	1219-1229	PAGO	548-586
MASM	50- 68	PAGO	593-604
MASM	77-103	RIAN	556-567
OPPO	223-239	SHLI	415-420
POPO	82- 90	TIMW	396-404
POSU	151-160		

Caesar, Julius

ROAG	61- 74		
		GAWA	ix-xviii
TILI	329-336(b)		
		HILL	88- 95
WIHO	255-264		
		LACL	99-174

Cabell, James Branch

		LIHRO	291-315
AFGT	114-123	LITC	3- 50(b)
AMFH	608-615		

Cahan, Abraham

AMNO	315-322		
		AMDA	87- 93
ARNO	261-267		
BIBM	291-325	Caillois, Roger	
CAAN	339-352	NELI	175-183
COAM	104-113		

Cain, James M.

COYE	335-340		
		NOVA	13- 22
MACA	335-345 v.3		
		TOGW	110-128
MIAN	41- 66		

Caldwell, Erskine

| | | AMDR | 121-128 |

Caldwell, Erskine (cont.)

    AMFI   219-249

    NOVA   106-123

Calhoun, John C.

    MACA   69- 82 v.2

Callaghan, Morley

    BIBM   515-525

Callimachus

    HIGL   702-717

Calpurnius Siculus, Titus

    LIHRS   264-277

Calvino, Italo

    GUCI   143-149

Camoens, Luís de

    ENEI   238-250

Campanella, Giovan Domenico

    HIIL   299-306

Campbell, Bartley

    HIAD   118-124 v.1

Campbell, John W.

    SETO   27- 46

Campbell, Joseph

    CLCO   182-189

Campton, David

    ANTH   159-166

Camus, Albert

    AGIN   52- 60

    CONT   291-296

    COTH   211-217

    DIPA   184-190

    FRLH   137-170

    FRPC   344-368

    INLI   207-218

    LIRE   167-174

    LYCE   5- 17

    LYCE   335-365

    MOFT   132-152

    MORL   87- 93

    NELI   103-117

    NEYT   174-180

    OCLI   306-321

    PISA   57-108

    PRVM   56- 82

REHV   276-283   HIOM   130-136

Canfield, Dorothy

   AMFH   706-714

   CAAN   294-299

Cantwell, Robert

   PRWT   75- 84

Čapek, Karel

   EXIN   208-224

Capote, Truman

   AFTE   138-145

   CRPR   94-107

   FIFO   237-243

   RAIS   230-258

   WWFS   283-299

   WOWE   285-296

Cardinal Newman see
   Newman, Cardinal

Cardozo, Benjamin N.

   BOTC   207-215

Carducci, Giosue

   HIIL   436-445

Carew, Thomas

   INPO   3- 8

Carey, Henry C.

   MACA   105-111 v. 3

Carleton, William

   CAEN   192-197

Carlyle, Thomas

   BRVL   357-379

   DROR   122-151

   ERGO   179-191

   HIOC   92-110

   LIHE   1309-1321

   LIHIC   1309-1321

   RIFM   26- 36

   VIDE   77- 89

Carpentier, Alejo

   INMA   37- 67

Carr, John Dickson

   MIAN   67- 80

Carroll, Lewis

   SHLI   540-550

Carson, Rachel

   BOTC   260-268

Caruthers, William A.

   MACA   41- 46 v. 2

   RIAN   276-284

Carver, Jonathon

   LIHA   141-150

Cary, Joyce

   CONE   131-147

   INENO   177-184

   LILC   151-156

   WWFS   51- 67

Casanova, Jacques

   WOBO   182-194

Cash, W. J.

   BOTC   229-238

Casona, Alejandro

   BASP   xi-xxiv(b)

   BASP   xx-xliii

Castelvetro, Lodovico

   HICR   80- 89

Castiglione, Baldassare

   HIIL   226-231

Cather, Willa

   AFGT   48- 56

   AMFH   683-697

   AMNF   144-153

   AMNO   281-293

   ARNO   255-261

   AWTC   54- 62

   CAAN   319-338

   CEOW   29- 39

   COAM   113-222

   COYE   527-533

   FERE   255-263

   FIMA   23- 62

   FIYA   69- 87

   FRWE   112-135

   LAPR   153-220

   PICA   92-122

   TWEN   181-190

Catullus, Gaius Valerius

HILL 79- 87

LIHRO 227-240

Celan, Paul

GEML 161-184

Céline, Louis-Ferdinand

DENE 56- 65

WWTS 83-102

Celsus, Aulus Cornelius

LIHRS 92-100

Cendrars, Blaise

BOML 58- 80

SEWB vii-x

SEWB 1- 44

WWTS 31- 56

Cervantes Saavedra, Miguel de

EISP xxvi-xxxiii

ENNO 9- 19

ENNO 279-288

HACR 88-143

LINL 440-445

LINO 74-107

LIWM 44- 50

TILI 221-239

Chamisso, Adelbert von

ESTD 240-258

Chandler, Raymond

BPSW 227-232(b)

CACL 371-380(b)

TOGW 171-185

Channing, William Ellery

FLNE 108-114

MACA 328-338 v. 2

Chaplin, Charles

KICA 55- 68

Chapman, George

SELE 58- 73

Chapman, John Jay

CONT 64- 69

TRTH 133-164

Char, René

GUCF 257-263

Chase, J. Smeaton
 CACL   197-206(b)

Chase, James Hadley
 COEC   216-224

Chateaubriand, François-
 René de
 FRLI   22- 36
 HICT   109-117
 HIMW   231-240

Chaucer, Geoffrey
 CHEL   41- 55
 COESA   8- 17
 CORE   24- 35 v.1
 CRAL   224-232
 GRCR   367-378
 HIEL   33- 40
 LIHE   249-263
 LIHI   249-263
 LINO   44- 73
 SELE   27- 44
 SHEL   116-130
 SHSE   64- 77
 TILI   240-249

 WIHO   127-136

Cheever, John
 AMSS   46- 55
 RAIS   188-194

Chekhov, Anton Pavlovich
 COTH   59-80
 DETR   300-306
 ESRN   234-247
 GRBR   309-345
 KICA   90- 96
 LAES   178-203
 MADR   508-520
 MIRO   251-262
 MOPW   114-152
 MYPO   175-181
 NEYT   126-132
 OURL   158-168
 PLAC   2- 11(b)
 PRTR   214-222
 RUNO   274-301
 SPTR   283-293

Chénier, André
 FRLI   62- 68

Chernyshevsky, Nikolay G.

   AMLI   222-238

   HIOM   238-245

Chesnutt, Charles Waddell

   MIAN   28- 40

   NEVA   34- 46

Chesterfield, Philip Dormer
   Stanhope, 4th Earl of

   COESA   80- 85

   CORE   89- 96 v.2

Chesterton, Gilbert Keith

   RIFM   219-226

Chestnut, Mary Boykin Miller

   PAGO   277-298

Chettle, Henry

   IDAE   202-210

Child, Lydia Maria (Francis)

   RIAN   177-184

Chopin, Kate

   AMEI   296-305

Churchill, Winston

COAM   47- 56

Cicero, Marcus Tullius

   BAWC   ix-xxii

   HICL   213-221

   HILL   108-139

   LACL   175-206

   LERBL   86-100

   LIHRO   255-290

   RHGR   68- 80

Cioran, E. M.

   NELI   213-223

   TEEX   11- 29

Clapp, Louisa Smith

   CACL   66- 76(b)

Clark, Walter Van Tilburg

   FIFO   310-324

   NOFI   170-196

Clark, William

   BOTC   14- 25

Clarke, Arthur

   SETO   374-391

Claudel, Paul

    ANGH   163-169

    COFP   71- 93

    DETR   333-341

    DIPA   127-145

    FRPC   122-141

    GUCF   89-118

    GUCF   173-178

    MOFT   69- 89

    PRTR   226-243

Claudian (Claudius
Claudianus)

    HILL   388-398

Cleaver, Eldridge

    BLAW   37- 49

    CONR   6- 12

Clemens, Samuel Langhorne
    see Twain, Mark

Cleland, Robert Glass

    CACL   257-267(b)

Cobb, John B., Jr.

    COPT   63- 71

Cobbett, William

    DROR   59- 82

Coccioli, Carlo

    SHGO   8- 17

Cocteau, Jean

    DIPA   74- 88

    GUCF   208-213

    MICF   116-123

    MOFT   48- 68

    WWTS   57- 81

Cody, William F.

    VILA   113-125

Coleridge, Samuel Taylor

    DROR   91- 98

    ESFD   92- 97

    HICT   200-233

    HIEL   301-307

    HIMW   151-187

    IMSC   76- 87

    IMSC   169-181

    INLA   115-133

    LASA   201-222

LIHE	1149-1158	CONE	201-219	
LIHIC	1149-1158	INENO	184-190	
LISH	339-357	LILC	170-175	
LISH	384-409	WROW	112-152	
OBCO	97-133			
OPRI	191-225	Congreve, William		
OTIN	10- 17	COES	76- 84	
SEES	198-305	FIMC	131-198	
		POSU	59- 72	
Colette		REDR	151-174	
CONTI	152-157	Connolly, Cyril		
IMTR	86-141	CLCO	280-285	
		IMSC	255-261	
Collins, Wilkie				
CAEN	234-243	Conrad, Joseph		
FAOR	296-305	APTC	108-152	
MUFP	36- 42	ARNO	184-195	
OPRI	255-270	CAEN	423-440	
		COES	302-313	
Columella, Lucius Junius Moderatus		CORE	309-318 v.1	
LIHRS	131-137	ENLT	125-136	
		ENNO	229-244	
Comfort, Alex		ENNO	440-454	
REHV	222-228	GRTR	173-226	
		INENO	67- 81	
Compton-Burnett, Ivy				

Conrad, Joseph (cont.)

LILC	178-185
LINL	190-199
MOBF	65-136
NOMW	26- 62
NOVE	156-172
PORE	13- 67
REND	336-348
SEES	31- 58
TRWO	148-169

Conroy, Jack

PRWT	85- 95

Constant, Benjamin

STHT	203-223

Cooke, John Esten

RIAN	463-472

Cooper, James Fenimore

AMFH	53- 76
AMNF	1- 12
AMNO	21- 42
AMSL	95-101
BEDA	39- 47

CAAN	14- 29
COOC	192-206
CYAL	39- 46
ETAN	6- 24
FRAL	27- 68
INDR	176-199
LIOA	226-235
LITR	94-102
LODA	170-212
MACA	222-237 v.2
MASM	226-254
RIAN	115-164
ROAL	76- 83
SHRE	582-594i
SHRE	941-966
STCA	37- 63
TWGA	1- 8
VILA	64- 76
WOEL	71-77
WOWI	167-182
WOWI	313-333

Copeau, Jacques

MOFT	243-249

Corbière, Tristan

    LIRE   60- 73

Corey, Lewis see
   Fraina, Louis C.

Corneille, Pierre

    CHPC   3- 49

    CLGR   37- 44

    DETR   54- 75

    EVPP   73- 88

    MADR   267-273

    SPTR   216-224

    STHT   105-115

Corso, Gregory

    ALWA   57- 64

    POOP   172-181

Cortázar, Julio

    INMA   206-245

Coward, Noël

    RIFW   124-145

Cowley, Abraham

    ENEI   421-427

    LICR   122-131

Cowper, William

    LIHE   1095-1102

    LIHIB   1095-1102

Cox, Harvey

    COPT   166-185

Cozzens, James Gould

    AMMO   145-150

    FIFO   150-171

    PUPN   143-151

    TWGA   160-176

Crabbe, George

    OPRI   165-190

Craddock, Charles Egbert
   see Murfree, Mary Noailles

Crane, Hart

    AMPP   494-511

    CLGR   128-138

    DAEC   121-140

    ESFD   310-323

    EVHO   63- 81

    EXRE   227-234

    FIMA   63-100

Crane, Hart (cont.)

HIAP	468-479
INDR	577-603
MASM	324-338
MOAM	272-298
MOPE	219-242
MOPO	153-164
MOPR	168-182
POOT	312-330
TWEN	257-274

Crane, Stephen

AMEI	185-205
AMFH	532-538
AMNF	86- 96
AMPP	240-249
CAAN	212-216
COYE	129-137
ETAN	115-123
FERE	227-235
LINL	232-237
LIOA	754-760
REAN	69-136
RORH	99-107(b)
SHAC	60- 76

TWDR	36- 42

Crapsey, Adelaide

HIAP	91- 97

Crawford, Francis Marion

AMEI	236-242
AMFH	385-403
CAAN	166-171

Creeley, Robert

ALWA	65- 74
AMPO	151-157

Crèvecoeur, Hector St. John de

COOC	73- 78
LIHAR	347-358
MACA	140-147 v.1
SHRE	927-938
STCA	23- 33

Crichton, Robert

AFTE	49- 63

Croce, Benedetto

LISH	500-519

Crosby, Henry G.

    EXRE   246-284

Crothers, Rachel

    HIAD   50- 61 v.2

Crouse, Russel

    MOAP   145-150(b)

Cruse, Harold

    BLAWP   227-239

Cruz, San Juan de la

    LAPO   79-121

Cruz, Juana Inés de la

    EPLA   33- 40

    SPAL   85- 92

Cummings, E. E.

    AMPP   511-525

    BABY   100-106

    DAEC   1- 29

    HIAP   336-347

    MOAM   249-271

    MOPR   145-152

    PLDO   159-194

POOT   111-116

POPO   143-150

SHRE   1247-1253

THBU   203-208

Cunningham, J. V.

    COCH   143-149

    JOJC   5- 40

    POOP   40- 47

    POPR   134-155

Curtis, George William

    MACA   147-154 v.3

    TIMW   11-19

Curtius, Quintus

    LIHRS   81- 91

Cynewulf

    LIHE   70- 75

    LIHI   70- 75

Dahlberg, Edward

    PRWT   64- 73

Dali, Salvador

    CLCO   190-195

Daly, Augustin

    HIAD   1- 38 v.1

Dame Shirley see Clapp,
   Louisa Smith

Dana, Richard Henry

    CACL   151-161(b)

    SHRE   1013-1030

    STCA   112-129

Daniel, Samuel

    ENEI   322-337

D'Annunzio, Gabriele

    MOIN   36- 50

    MORL   126-132

Dante Alighieri

    DICO   iii-xiii

    DIVC   50-98(b)v.10

    DIVC   208-303 v.10

    ESFD   424-446

    HICL   416-446

    HIIL   41- 72

    HIWL   49- 58

    LICR   80- 87

    NOIT   21- 39

    SEWS   251-269

    SPLE   50- 99

    TILI   128-153

    TOCC   125-135

    VINU   vii-xxii

    WIHO   89-105

Darió, Rubén

    EPLA   103-110

Darwin, Charles

    VIDE   309-316

Da Verona, Guido

    MOIN   80- 86

Davies, Sir John

    OPPO   149-155

Davies, Joseph E.

    CLCO   98-104

Davis, Ossie

    BLAWP   144-150

Davis, Rebecca Harding

    AMFH   181-190

42

Davis, Richard Harding

AMEI	174-184
AMFH	525-532
COYE	100-106

Dawson, Edward

| POMI | 34- 39 |

Day, Thomas

| LINL | 28- 39 |

De Camp, L. Sprague

| SETO | 151-166 |

Defoe, Daniel

ASPN	88- 95
BEJA	22- 42
CAEN	31- 40
CHEL	108-114
COES	62- 75
CORE	125-135 v.1
CORE	50- 58 v.2
ENNO	33- 43
ENNO	296-307
FAOR	216-258
INEN	55- 62

LIHE	847-856
LIHIB	847-865
NOVE	23- 38
REND	3- 22
RINO	61-134
TILI	297-321
WOVN	38- 46
WOWE	49- 60

De Forest, John William

AMFH	166-174
AMNF	35- 46
MIAN	10- 27
PAGO	669-742
RIAN	505-520

De La Cruz, San Juan
    see Cruz, San Juan de la

de la Mare, Walter

CAEN	533-546
ESFI	33- 45
LILC	210-215
POAG	135-140

Deland, Margaretta Wade
    Campbell

| AMFH | 459-470 |

Delaney, Shelagh

    ANTH   109-118

Deledda, Grazia

    MOIN   57- 73

Dell, Floyd

    COAM   166-171

Deloney, Thomas

    IDAE   238-280

Del Rey, Lester

    SETO   167-186

Demby, William

    NASO   173-189

    NENO   191-196

Demetillo, Ricaredo

    NEWP   113-119

Democritus

    HIGL   335-340

Demosthenes

    ANCR   278-285

    ECGR   107-114

    HIGL   596-607

    HIGR   176-181

Dennis, Nigel

    THPP   261-267

De Quincey, Thomas

    COES   165-172

    COESB   1- 7

    CORE   141-149 v. 2

    HIOC   110-120

    OPRI   101-131

    OPRI   226-254

De Sanctis, Francesco

    HIOM   97-124

Descartes, René

    STHT   50- 72

De Voto, Bernard

    FRWE   136-152

Dickens, Charles

    AGFI   105-175

    ARFI   136-161

    ARNO   117-124

44

BRVL	243-252	REND	131-151
CAEN	213-236	STCL	26- 38
CHEL	156-163	STCL	137-155
COEA	413-460	TILI	363-368
CRAL	365-370	TIPI	126-136
ENNO	125-138	VIDE	101-125
ENNO	370-379	VILI	121-158
ESFI	61- 78	VINO	22- 59
EXNO	32- 40	WOBO	1-104
EXNO	49- 81	WOVN	169-185
EXNO	107-131	WOVN	197-225
FAOR	306-317	WOVN	260-279
GRTR	227-248	WOVN	337-351
IMSC	182-202		
INEN	123-138	Dickey, James	
KICA	3- 17	ALWA	75- 98
LIHE	1344-1351	POOP	225-238
LIHIC	1344-1351	Dickinson, Emily	
LINL	82- 87	AMPP	181-222
LIWM	228-234	COCH	100-127
MIRO	70- 82	CONT	50- 56
NOVE	191-207	CYAL	164-169
OPSE	50- 65	ESFD	281-298
PSLP	25- 65	INDR	283-299

45

Dickinson, Emily (cont.)

    LIOA   729-736

    MAPO   88- 94

    MOAM   18- 39

    POEX   91-114

    POMI   90-104

    ROAL   257-263

Dickinson, John

    LIHA   234-241

    LIHAR   21- 34

    MACA   219-232 v.1

Diderot, Denis

    HICT   89- 97

    HIMC   46- 61

    STHT   185-202

Dilthey, Wilhelm

    HIOM   320-335

Dinesen, Isak

    IMTR   149-163

Dionysius of Halicarnassus

    HICL   127-137

Disraeli, Benjamin

    CAEN   180-187

    DROR   167-183

    LINL   75- 80

    VIDE   127-133

Dobie, J. Frank

    BPSW   193-203

Döblin, Alfred

    DIMN   99-137

Dobrolyubov, Nikolay

    HIOM   245-253

Donleavy, J. P.

    COAN   149-154

    RAIS   194-200

Donne, John

    COES   32- 45

    CORE   20- 37 v.2

    ESFD   239-252

    MASM   3- 49

    POMI   3- 32

    SELE   106-125

    WEWU   11-18

Doolittle, Hilda

    HIAP   192-200

Dos Passos, John

AFGT	134-146
AMFI	25- 66
AMMO	65- 90
AWTC	136-142
CAAN	382-389
FIFO	119-125
FIYA	151-164
INLA	49- 62
LIBN	140-145
MONA	150-155
NOAM	163-194
NOVA	23- 51
PRWT	46- 63
RANU	155-164
SHLI	429-435
SHLI	446-450
THBU	212-219
TWGA	87-103
WRIC	89-139

Dostoyevsky, Anna G.

    EXRE   84-90

Dostoyevsky, Fedor

ARFI	245-271
ASPN	184-195
ESRN	130-169
GRBR	136-233
LASS	271-279
LINL	406-412
LINO	310-319
LIWM	246-251
MIRO	199-222
MYPO	106-174
OURL	130-144
RUNO	159-204
RUTH	78-190
STCL	9- 29
STCL	136-155
TILI	404-410(b)

Douglas, Norman

    LILC   223-233

Doyle, Sir Arthur Conan

    CLCO   266-274

    EXIN   157-171

Doyle, Sir Arthur Conan (cont.)

FAOR	22- 45
MUFP	45- 61

Dreiser, Theodore

AFGT	21- 27
AMEI	334-345
AMFH	645-652
AMNF	106-116
AMNO	245-259
ARNO	244-254
CAAN	281-293
COAM	74- 83
CONT	87- 99
COYE	294-313
CYAL	224-230
DENE	137-150
ETAN	124-132
FERE	235-244
FIMA	101-138
FIYA	33- 47
INDA	218-227(b)
LODA	241-248
MACA	354-359 v.3
MAWH	153-165

MONA	44- 56
REAN	287-379
ROAL	309-314
SHRE	1160-1208
WOEL	235-252

Drury, Allen

PUPN	187-193

Dryden, John

DETR	39- 44
ENEI	465-481
HICR	371-391
HIEL	158-165
LICR	88-104
LIHE	722-732
LIHIB	722-732
LISH	182-193
LISH	196-217
REDR	19- 62
SELE	187-194
SHEL	472-477

Duché, Jacob

LIHAR	286-294

Dudintsev, Vladimir

    HISL   317-327

Dugan, Alan

    ALWA   99-106

Duhamel, Georges

    FRPC   173-200

Dulany, Daniel

    LIHA   102-110

Dumas, Alexandre

    FAOR   267-276

Dunbar, Paul Laurence

    BLAW   111-124

    NENO   38- 43

    NEVA   46- 56

Duncan, Robert

    AMPO   145-151

    POOP   133-146

Dunlap, William

    HIAM   74-112

    WOWI   119-137

Dunne, Finley Peter

    RIFA   178-190

Duras, Marguerite

    NEFN   85- 91

Durrell, Lawrence

    CONE   40- 61

    FABU   17- 28

    INTE   82- 90

    LASI   280-287

    LINL   303-309

    OCLI   322-329

    POBF   215-222

    WWSS   257-282

Dürrenmatt, Friedrich

    THPP   134-161

Eastman, Max

    CLCO   57- 69

Eberhart, Richard

    COAP   9- 31

Eberhart, Richard (cont.)

    POOP   17- 39

    POPR   73- 91

Echegaray y Eizaguirre,
  José

    SODJ   5- 23

Edgeworth, Maria

    BEJA   319-330

    LINL   39- 45

Edwards, Jonathan

    COOC   40- 46

    LIOA   106-116

    LITR   46- 52

    MACA   152-163 v. 1

Eggleston, Edward

    RIAN   538-556

    VILA   271-283

Ehrenburg, Ilya

    HISL   110-123

    SORL   208-217

    VOSN   105-140(b)

Eich, Günter

GEML   89-107

Elder, Lonne

    BLAWP   219-226

Eliot, George

    AGFI   253-293

    ARNO   146-151

    BRVL   215-242

    CAEN   319-335

    CHEL   136-146

    COES   196-204

    CONTI   138-148

    CORE   229-242 v. 1

    ENNO   171-181

    ENNO   401-409

    GRTR   28-125

    HENR   98-115

    INEN   171-190

    LINL   94-109

    MOWO   168-173

    NOVE   127-140

    REND   197-214

    VIDE   284-296

    VILI   182-209

VINO	262–307		INDI	35– 60
WOVN	298–321		INDR	460–501
WOVN	351–371		INLI	90–101
WRWC	50– 75		LASS	345–350
			LASS	430–436

Eliot, Thomas Stearns

			LIBN	156–163
AMLA	288–310		LILC	254–270
AMPP	414–427		LISH	664–678
AWTC	203–211		LITR	282–290
AWTC	306–316		MAPO	373–379
AXCA	93–131		MASM	302–323
BIBM	364–402		MOAM	222–248
CLGR	146–154		MOPE	176–200
COEB	236–242		MOPE	301–316
CONTI	69– 77		MOPO	59– 68
COTH	143–169		MOPR	75–103
COYE	586–599		MYPO	185–192
CYAL	278–286		NEYT	139–145
DAEC	184–218		ORUN	241–266
ENLT	323–329		PLDO	39–117
ESFD	462–470		POMI	105–124
EXRE	110–115		POOT	152–180
FIMA	139–174		POPO	135–142
HIAP	419–428		POPO	293–300
IMSC	262–294			

Eliot, Thomas Stearns (cont.)

POPO	323-329
PORE	131-189
RIFM	233-239
SHLI	436-441
SPTR	293-301
TEAH	222-228
TWEN	330-343
WAFE	216-224
WWSS	89-110

Elliott, George P.

AFTE	125-137
REHV	37- 43

Ellison, Ralph

AMDA	177-186
AMDA	188-196
BLAW	143-168
LANI	68- 86
NASO	127-148
NENO	196-212
OCLI	330-346
RAIS	168-178
REAM	19- 24

SHAC	3- 23
SHAC	167-183
STCL	118-123
WWSS	317-334

Eluard, Paul

COFP	125-151
MICF	170-175
SELW	vii-xxxvi

Emerson, Ralph Waldo

AMPP	90-114
AMRE	3- 75
AMSL	144-152
BEDA	57- 69
CONT	41- 47
COOC	234-255
EVHO	28- 43
FLNE	203-216
FLNE	261-276
FLNE	300-306
FLNE	545-550
HENR	116-138
HIOC	163-176
INDR	577-603

LASA	186-200	Ennius, Quintus	
LOIA	276-291	HILL	21-28
LIOA	397-408	LIHRO	100-113
LITR	136-155		
MACA	386-399 v.2	Enzensberger, Hans Magnus	
MASM	271-280	GEML	239-258
NEYT	63- 69	Epictetus	
POHC	235-242	DIEP	xi-xlv
POPO	98-105		
REAP	35- 59	Epicurus	
ROAL	121-130	ANCR	252-260
SEPP	v-xix	Erasmus, Desiderius	
SHRE	600-658	HICR	10- 16
WAFE	209-215		
WOEL	63- 70	Essenin, Sergey	
		SORL	11- 18

Emmanuel, Pierre

Etherege, Sir George

COFP	95-114	FIMC	20- 37
MICF	253-259	FIMC	86- 95

Empson, William

		REDR	63-103
CRAL	303-312	Euripides	
LILC	274-280	ANCR	190-195
MODP	55- 63	FRSS	29- 35
MODP	177-187	GRWA	271-283

Euripides (cont.)

   HIGL   360-404

   HIGR   91- 98

   LAGL   147-159

   MADR   56- 78

   SPTR   103-125

   TILI   64- 69(b)

Evans, Donald

   HIAP   255-263

Evelyn, John

   COESA   44- 50

Everett, Edward

   FLNE   75- 91

Everson, William see
   Antoninus, Brother

Evtushenko, Evgeny

   VOSN   78- 89(b)

Exton, Clive

   ANTH   203-213

Falkner, J. Meade

   LINL   213-219

Farmer, P. J.

   SETO   392-409

Farrell, James T.

   AMFI   287-305

   FIYA   237-256

   MONA   155-160

   NOAM   195-225

   NOVA   69- 85

Fast, Howard

   RANU   275-286

Faulkner, William

   AMDA   129-135

   AMFI   123-169

   AMMO   91-106

   AMNF   219-228

   APTC   79-107

   AWTC   263-274

   BLAW   93- 98

   CAAN   417-425

   CLCO   460-470

   CONT   130-158

   CYAL   291-300

   ETAN   163-176

EVHO	175-196	STCL	47- 66
EVPP	159-173	STCL	137-155
FIFO	178-186	TEAH	171-184
FIMA	175-210	TWGA	142-159
FIYA	165-182	VAHE	73-111
INLI	13- 27	WOEL	78- 84
LASA	496-506	WRIC	143-183
LITR	318-323	WWFS	119-141
LODA	309-315		

Fauset, Jessie Redmon

LODA	443-449

NEVA 131-139

LUGD	56- 77

LYCE	311-320

Fedin, Konstantin

MONA	168-180

SORL 130-139

NOAM	75-109

Feierberg, Mordekhai Ze'ev

NOIT	111-118

MATM 46-56

NOVA	144-166

PISA	179-219

Feldman, Irving

PRVM	110-135

ALWA 107-115

PUPN	170-175

Fellini, Federico

REAP	167-195

JUSI 1- 7

RIFA	347-353

JUSI 11- 65

RIFA	404-409

SEES	59- 79

Fénelon, François

SEMA	118-152

ENEI 484-493

Ferber, Edna

    PUPN   48- 57

Ferrero, Leo

    SPLE   180-198

Fiedler, Leslie A.

    LASS   398-404

    MYPO   209-217

Field, Edward

    ALWA   116-130

Fielding, Henry

    ARFI   33- 54

    ARNO   52- 67

    BEJA   103-130

    CAEN   58- 68

    CLRE   212-217

    ENNO   65- 81

    ENNO   322-336

    INEN   45- 51

    INEN   71- 81

    LIHE   955-961

    LIHIB   955-961

    LINL   3- 11

    LIWM   90- 95

    NOVE   59- 74

    REND   42- 57

    RINO   248-289

Finkel, Donald

    ALWA   131-144

Firbank, Ronald

    CLCO   486-502

Fishback, Margaret

    FAAH   25- 34

Fisher, Dorothy Canfield
    see Canfield, Dorothy

Fiske, John

    MACA   203-211 v.3

Fitch, Clyde

    HIAD   265-296 v.1

Fitzgerald, Edward

    RUOK   4- 15(b)

Fitzgerald, F. Scott

    AMDA   107-128

    AMNF   180-191

56

BIBM	16- 27(b)	PAGO	341-364
BIBM	515-525	Flaccus, Gaius Valerius	
ETAN	152-160	LIHRS	346-360
EXNO	133-162		
FIMA	211-238	Flaubert, Gustave	
FIYA	135-149	ARFI	163-188
INTE	98-105	ESFD	131-140
LAPR	287-352	FAOR	259-267
MASM	154-159	FLJB	1- 29
MONA	130-142	FRLI	298-305
NEYT	154-161	HIOM	6- 12
NOAM	45- 74	LICR	262-267
SEMA	81-117	MIRO	184-196
SEST	94-108	NEYT	113-119
SHLI	27- 35	NOFI	197-214
TEAH	157-170	OPSE	173-205
TIPI	56- 74	ROAG	152-164
TWEN	126-143	STHT	248-261
TWGA	104-119	TILI	379-390
WITS	137-146	TRTH	72- 87
		WROW	72- 94

FitzGerald, R. D.

ESPO	122-141	Fletcher, John Gould	
		HIAP	201-206

Fitzhugh, George

Fletcher, Joseph

    COPT   185-196

Flexner, Abraham

    BOTC   152-164

Flint, Timothy

    FRWE   39- 54

    RIAN   213-223

Fogazzaro, Antonio

    MOIN   29- 36

Fontane, Theodor

    ESTD   287-306

    GENO   178-214

Fontenelle, Bernard Le Bovier
  de

    STHT   139-148

Ford, Ford Madox

    HERT   175-182

    LILC   300-305

    LINL   251-263

    MOBF   137-175

    WOWE   97-104

Forster, E. M.

    COES   342-351

    IMSC   295-310

    INENO   152-163

    LASA   223-238

    LINL   244-250

    LILC   306-318

    MOBF   176-224

    MOWO   47- 55

    WWFS   23- 35

Foscolo, Ugo

    HIIL   378-385

    HIMW   265-272

Fowler, Gene

    CLCO   133-139

Fowles, John

    AFTE   161-175

    SEST   28- 38

Fraina, Louis C.

    PRWT   194-221

France, Anatole

    LINL   359-364

TILI	430-452

Franklin, Benjamin

COOC	78- 94
LIHAR	359-381
LIOA	116-123
MACA	164-178 v.1
STCA	9- 21

Frederic, Harold

AMEI	206-219
TIPI	75- 95

Freeman, Mary Wilkins

AMFH	433-440
DEAS	317-323

Freneau, Philip

COOC	123-130
LIHA	171-183
LIHA	413-424
LIHAR	246-276
LIOA	165-171
MACA	368-381 v.1

Freud, Sigmund

BEYC	89-118

CONT	353-362
CONT	377-382
ESTD	411-428
LASA	63- 80
LASS	150-167
MOTB	585-591
MOWO	78- 95
TWDR	60- 68

Frisch, Max

SEST	57- 74
THPP	161-183

Frontinus, Sextus Julius

LIHRS	338-345

Frost, Robert

AMPP	293-327
BABY	200-209
BEDA	116-142
COCH	160-189
FIMA	239-273
HIAP	150-162
MAWH	201-212
MOAM	60- 91
MOPO	49- 58

Frost, Robert (cont.)

    MOPE   485-500

    NEYT   146-153

    POAG   26- 62

    POOT   61- 78

    SEES   118-136

    WWSS   7- 34

Fuchs, Daniel

    PRWT   96-105

Fuentes, Carlos

    INMA   276-309

Fuller, Henry Blake

    AMEI   107-116

    AMFH   424-432

    COYE   167-179

Fuller, Margaret

    FLNE   244-250

    MACA   426-434 v.2

Fuller, Roy

    MODP   23-31

Gaboriau, Emile

    MUFP   30- 36

Gaiser, Gerd

    COEN   91-100

    GEML   111-138

Galbraith, John Kenneth

    BOTC   251-259

Gale, Zona

    AMFH   700-706

Galloway, Joseph

    LIHA   370-383

Galsworthy, John

    AMBL   220-226

    ARNO   206-216

    CAEN   477-493

    ENLT   163-182

    INENO   95-100

    LINL   282-288

    MOPW   204-225

    REND   320-335

Galt, John

    LINL   46- 51

Garcia Lorca, Féderico

    COTH   242-258

    GYBA   11- 17

    MORL   172-178

    PONY   ix-xxxix

    PONY   181-192

García Márquez, Gabriel

    INMA   310-341

Gardner, Isabella

    COAP   122-133

Garland, Hamlin

    AMEI   93-106

    AMFH   454-459

    CAAN   205-212

    COAM   39- 47

    COYE   165-172

    MACA   288-300 v.3

    VILA   284-290

    WOWE   243-253

Garrigue, Jean

    AMPO   80- 92

Garrison, William Lloyd

    MACA   352-361 v.2

Garson, Barbara

    CONR   234-247

Gascoigne, George

    IDAE   97-109

Gaskell, Elizabeth Cleghorn
  Stevenson

    CAEN   251-260

    VIDE   132-138

    VINO   183-226

Gass, William

    AFTE   95-105

    CONR   70- 79

Gathorne-Hardy, Robert

    BIBM   124-130

Gautier, Judith

    ROAG   202-210

Genet, Jean

    FOPP   135-174

    INTE   116-130

    MADE   7- 31

    META   76- 83

Genet, Jean (cont.)

    MORL   182-188

    OCLI   347-365

    THAB   140-167

    THPP   113-133

George, Henry

    MACA   125-136 v.3

Gernsback, Hugo

    EXIN   225-242

Gervinus, Georg

    HIOC   204-212

Ghelderode, Michel de

    SEPL   3- 26

    THPP   98-113

Gibbon, Edward

    COES   115-123

    ENEI   510-527

Gide, André

    APTC   153-181

    ASPN   146-153

    DIPA   159-165

    FRLH   49-134

    FRPC   71- 95

    GUCF   50- 88

    INLI   138-149

    LICA   129-173

    WHNO   v-xii

Gilbert, William S.

    CLCO   359-365

Gillette, William

    HIAD   212-238 v.1

Gilpin, William

    VILA   38- 46

Ginsberg, Allen

    ALWA   145-152

    AMPO   166-174

    WAFE   241-248

    WWTS   279-320

Ginzburg, Natalia

    GUCI   135-143

Giono, Jean

    BOML   100-120

Giraudoux, Jean

    COTH   194-201

    DIPA   59- 73

    FRSS   50- 55

    MOFT   19- 47

    THPL   vii-xiv

Gissing, George

    AGFI   343-348

    CAEN   406-411

    COED   428-436

    CORE   238-244 v. 2

    LINL   154-160

Glasgow, Ellen

    AMFH   670-682

    CAAN   267-280

    COYE   335-345

    FIYA   49- 68

    MONA   71- 82

    PICA   56- 91

    REAN   219-283

Glaspell, Susan

    MOAP   26- 49

Gnessin, Uri Nissan

    MATM   55- 80

Godkin, Edwin Lawrence

    MACA   154-168 v. 3

Godwin, Mary Wollstonecraft

    BEJA   309-314

Godwin, William

    BEJA   296-309

Goethe, Johann Wolfgang von

    DETR   166-172

    ERGO   1- 16

    ERGO   81-132

    ESTD   3- 92

    EVPD   89-106

    FRSB   15- 29

    GENO   3- 29

    GOFA   7- 57

    HICT   361-377

    HIGE   173-190

    HIMC   201-226

    LAES   96-140

    LASA   139-184

Goethe, Johann Wolfgang von (cont.)		Golding, William	
		CONE	254-260
LIWM	130-138	CONTI	186-194
MADR	326-334	LASI	289-294
OPPO	240-264	LINL	310-315
POPO	315-322	OCLI	366-387
TILI	322-328	POBF	196-206

Gogol, Nikolai Vasilévich		Goldoni, Carlo	
ESRN	35- 61	HIIL	343-352
GRBR	26- 49		
LASS	196-201	Goldsmith, Oliver	
MIRO	97-110	COEC	268-273
MYPO	98-105	COES	106-114
OURL	57- 70	LIHE	1056-1062
RUNO	64-102	LIHIB	1056-1062

Gold, Herbert		Goncharov, Ivan Alexandrovich	
COAN	170-181	GRBR	50- 63
CRPR	224-232	LINL	397-406
RAIS	180-187	RUNO	103-118

Gold, Michael		Góngora, Luis de	
PRWT	221-251	LAPO	27- 75
		PONY	167-177

Golden, Harry	
REHV	50- 70

Gonzalez, N. V. M.

    NEWP   42- 55

Goodman, Paul

    ALWA   153-163

    LIRE   187-198

    REHV   211-216

Gordon, Caroline

    FIFO   185-193

Gordon, William

    LIHAR   423-428

Gorey, Edward

    BIBM   479-484

Gorki, Maxim

    COTH   111-127

    ESRN   215-233

    GRBR   364-392

    HISL   1- 8

    LINL   426-433

    LIWM   362-367

    MADR   526-533

    OURL   192-198

Gosse, Sir Edmund

    COESB   81- 87

    LINL   148-154

Gotta, Salvatore

    MOIN   233-241

Gotthelf, Jeremias

    GENO   101-142

Gower, John

    SHSE   58- 64

Graham, Sheilah

    BIBM   16- 27

Grant, Ulysses Simpson

    PAGO   131-173

Grass, Günter

    COEN   109-124

    GEML   215-235

    LASI   110-117

    REHV   199-204

    STCL   123-128

Graves, Robert

    LILC   369-375

Gray, Thomas

    POPO   278-285

Grayson, William J.

    MACA   103-108 v. 2

Greeley, Horace

    MACA   247-258 v. 2

Green, Henry

    CONE   183-200

    INENO   190-196

Greene, Graham

    CONE   87-106

    INENO   170-177

    LILC   378-385

    LUGD   111-123

    PISA   220-274

    PRVM   136-157

    SHGO   41- 65

    VAHE   45- 72

Greene, Robert

    IDAE   138-156

    LIHE   421-428

    LIHIA   421-428

    SHSE   139-144

Greenough, Horatio

    AMRE   140-152

Grenier, Jean

    LYCE   326-331

Gresham, William Lindsay

    TOGW   218-224

Grierson, Francis

    PAGO   70- 91

Griffin, John Howard

    AMMO   251-265

Griggs, Sutton E.

    NEVA   56- 67

Guillén, Jorge

    CANT   1- 12

Guimarães Rosa, João

    FISL   8- 13

    INMA   137-172

Guiney, Louise Imogen

    HIAP   83- 91

Guiterman, Arthur

    FAAH   35- 43

Gunn, Thom

    MODP   17- 22

H. D. see Doolittle, Hilda

Haggard, Rider

    BOML   81- 99

    BOML   140-146

Hale, Edward E.

    EXIN   90- 98

Hallas, Richard

    TOGW   163-170

Hamilton, Alexander

    MACA   292-307 v.1

Hamilton, Edmond

    SETO   66- 83

Hammett, Dashiell

    TOGW   19- 29

    TOGW   61- 71

    TOGW   80-109

Hansberry, Lorraine

    BLAWP   157-170

Hardy, Thomas

    AGFI   295-322

    ARNO   164-171

    BRVL   267-280

    CAEN   352-372

    CEOW   3- 13

    CHEL   163-172

    COES   256-266

    CORE   266-280 v.2

    ENNO   195-209

    ENNO   418-427

    ESFD   329-340

    HACR   50- 70

    INENO   49- 62

    LIHE   1464-1474

    LIHIC   1464-1474

    LILI   7- 17

    MIRO   237-250

    MOBF   10- 64

    MOPE   150-175

    NOVE   141-155

    POOT   1- 11

Hardy, Thomas (cont.)

    REIM   95-111

    REND   237-249

    VILI   210-224

    WOVN   404-424

    WRWC   26- 49

Harrigan, Edward

    HIAD   82- 96 v.1

Harris, Frank

    COYE   250-255

Harris, Joel Chandler

    AMFH   374-384

    DEAS   277-283

    TIMW   378-387

Harris, Mark

    AFTE   65- 79

Hart, Moss

    MOAP   154-167(b)

Harte, Bret

    AMFH   232-242

    CACL   77- 90(b)

DEAS   220-241

RORH   47- 52(b)

SHSE   288-298

TIMW   266-290

Harvey, Gabriel

    COESA   33- 43

Hauptmann, Gerhart

    FRSS   80- 90

    MADR   452-466

    OCDR   152-164

Hauser, Arnold

    LASS   358-368

Hawkes, John

    COAN   192-204

    FABU   59- 94

Hawthorne, Nathaniel

    AMFH   132-148

    AMNF   13- 24

    AMNO   58- 83

    AMRE   179-368

    AMSL   144-152

    BEYC   179-208

CAAN	38- 57	RIAN	327-362
COOC	207-219	ROAL	140-148
CYAL	79- 88	SHRE	156-169
DEAS	91-110	SHRE	188-204
ETAN	24- 34	SHRE	427-565(b)
FLNE	217-235	SHRE	984-1011
FLNE	286-294	SHSE	246-263
FRAL	69-131	STCA	83-100
FRAL	350-375	TRWO	77- 96
HENR	42- 74	TWGA	9- 18
INDR	157-175	WOEL	93-124
LASS	55- 75		

Hazaz, Haiyim

    MATM   169-177

LASS	422-429		
LICR	328-340		

LIOA	308-321	Hazlitt, William	
LITR	114-128	COES	155-164
LODA	222-232	CORE	186-199 v. 2
LODA	417-479	HICT	251-266
LODA	485-519	HIMW	188-212
MACA	442-450 v. 2		

Hearn, Lafcadio

MAWH	3- 34	AMPH	509-516
OTIN	47- 65	COYE	232-246
POBL	34-102	MAWH	100-115
REAP	61- 85	RORH	74- 83(b)

Hebbel, Friedrich

    ERGO   133-146

Hecht, Anthony

    ALWA   164-173

Hegel, Georg

    HIMW   318-334

Heine, Heinrich

    COSG   140-169

    HIOC   192-201

Heinlein, Robert A.

    SETO   187-212

Heller, Joseph

    COAN   134-142

Hellman, Lillian

    MOAP   168-185

    WWTS   115-140

Héloise

    CLGR   29- 36

Helper, Hinton Rowan

    PAGO   365-379

Hemingway, Ernest

    AFGT   147-158

    AMFI   69-119

    AMMO   54- 64

    AMNF   192-205

    AWTC   185-195

    BIBM   515-525

    CAAN   368-381

    CLCO   3- 8

    CONTI   161-167

    CYAL   269-274

    ETAN   145-152

    FIMA   275-300

    FIYA   183-196

    FSFH   155-216

    INLI   28- 42

    KAFK   75- 83

    LASS   351-357

    MONA   94-111

    MYPO   193-201

    NEYT   162-168

    NOVA   166-198

    SEES   80-118

    SEMA   153-188

SHLI	339-344	ERGO	61- 80	
SHLI	613-629	HIMC	181-200	
TEAH	133-146			
TEAH	233-247	Herford, Oliver		
THBU	219-225	FAAH	44- 52	
TOGW	19- 50	Hergesheimer, Joseph		
TWEN	89- 97	AMFH	615-622	
TWEN	102-107	CAAN	306-311	
TWGA	120-141	COAM	122-131	
VAHE	112-145			
WOBO	214-242	Hernández, José		
WOWE	317-324	EPLA	145-151	
WRIC	39- 85	Herne, James A.		
WWSS	215-240	HIAD	129-162 v.1	
Hennequin, Emile		Herodotus		
HIOM	91- 96	ANCR	210-215	
		ENEI	41- 51	
Henry, Alexander		GRWA	159-182	
REVA	109-119	HIGL	306-327	
		HIGR	111-118	
Henry, O.				
COYE	264-274	LAGL	163-176	
DEAS	357-364			
		Herrick, Robert		
Herder, Johann Gottfried		CAAN	235-244	

71

Herrick, Robert (cont.)

    COAM   56- 65

    HACR   166-173

    WEWU   67- 75

Hersey, John

    AMMO   180-186

Herzen, Alexander

    GRBR   114-122

Hesiod

    HIGL   91-105

    HIGR   34- 42

Hettner, Hermann

    HIOM   292-297

Hildreth, Richard

    RIAN   292-300

Hillyer, Robert Silliman

    MOMP   84- 92

Himes, Chester

    NASO   87-101

Hindemith, Paul

    MOWO   174-183

Hine, Daryl

    ALWA   174-186

Hippocrates

    HIGL   485-492

Hirschbein, Peretz

    YILI   262-287

Hochwälder, Fritz

    THPP   184-195

Hoffenstein, Samuel Goodman

    FAAH   53- 60

Hoffman, Daniel

    ALWA   187-199

Hoffman, Frederick J.

    NOIT   153-160

Hofmannsthal, Hugo von

    FRSS   140-146

Holberg, Ludvig

    GESC   539-547

Hölderlin, Johann Christian Friedrich

    COSG   3- 65

ERGO	148-160		LERBL	428-443
			LICR	522-537
Hollander, John			SPTR	37- 47
ALWA	201-231		TILI	12- 33
			WIHO	19- 29
Holmes, Oliver Wendell				
AMPP	53- 59		Hood, Thomas	
BIBM	78-100		LINL	67- 74
BOTC	69- 77			
COESB	44- 50		Hooker, Thomas	
COOC	284-291		MACA	53- 62 v.1
FLNE	353-360			
FLNE	491-511		Hope, Alec Derwent	
LIOA	361-373		ESPO	142-157
MACA	451-459 v.2		Hopkins, Gerard Manley	
PAGO	743-796		AMRE	584-592
RIAN	494-504		BRVL	160-171
			INLA	63- 73
Homer			LILI	41- 46
ANCR	138-147		MOPO	73- 79
CLRE	7- 16		ORUN	78- 89
ENEI	21- 39		POOT	286-306
HIGL	14- 78		VILI	225-240
HIGR	16- 27			
LAGL	22- 53		Hopkins, Stephen	
LASI	171-187		LIHA	64- 74

Hopkinson, Francis

    LIHA   163-170

    LIHA   279-292

    LIHAR   131-157

Horace

    HICL   221-230

    HILL   164-183

    LIHRO   363-398

    LISH   77- 94

    POPO   221-227

    TILI   119-127

    WIHO   56- 64

Housman, Alfred Edward

    LILI   46- 52

    MOPE   140-149

    POOT   12- 18

    POPO   114-121

    TRTH   60- 71

Howard, Bronson

    HIAD   39- 64 v.1

Howard, Sidney

    AMDR   54- 60

Howe, Irving

    REHV   133-141

Howells, William Dean

    AMEI   24- 49

    AMFH   257-278

    AMNF   73- 85

    CAAN   127-144

    ETAN   67- 79

    FERE   50- 61

    HIAD   66- 81 v.1

    HIOM   206-212

    LIOA   665-680

    LITR   205-210

    MACA   241-253 v.3

    OPSE   76-103

    RIAN   653-701

    SHRE   570-579

    TWDR   43- 56

Howes, Barbara

    POOP   58- 71

Hoyt, Charles H.

    HIAD   96-103 v.1

Hudson, W. H.

   AMBL   295-301

Hufano, Alejandrino

   NEWP   119-125

Hughes, Langston

   BLAW   82-108
   BLAWP   77- 87

Hugo, Richard

   ALWA   232-246

Hugo, Victor

   DETR   161-166
   FRLI   129-156
   HIMW   252-258
   LINL   353-359
   TILI   344-351

Humboldt, Karl Wilhelm von

   ERGO   17- 45

Huneker, James Gibbons

   COYE   148-157
   RORH   86- 92(b)

Hurd, Richard

HICT   72- 80

Hurston, Zora Neale

   NENO   126-132

Husserl, Edmund

   LICA   21- 54

Hutchinson, Thomas

   LIHAR   394-411
   MACA   194-206 v.1

Huxley, Aldous

   ARNO   278-293
   CACL   357-369(b)
   CLCO   81- 86
   CLCO   209-214
   LILI   69- 78
   VAHE   3- 23
   WWSS   193-214

Ibsen, Henrik

   CONR   172-204
   COTH   8- 41
   CRID   81- 93
   DETR   290-298
   GESC   78- 83

GESC	555-582	Irving, Washington	
LIFD	54- 59	AMFH	40- 45
LIWM	284-291	AMSL	90- 95
MADR	354-383	COOC	152-165
MOPW	1- 51	CYAL	30- 35
OCDR	62- 88	DEAS	1- 26
PRTR	192-213	FRWE	58- 69
REHP	1- 34	LIOA	211-219
SPTR	260-274	MACA	203-212 v. 2
		REVA	53- 61
Imlay, Gilbert		ROAL	68- 75
RIAN	38- 43	WOWI	127-137(b)
		WOWI	152-166
Inge, William		WOWI	284-292
AMDS	41- 49		
MOAP	264-272		
		Isocrates	
Ionesco, Eugène		ANCR	268-274
AGIN	115-123	ECGR	63- 79
DIPA	229-237	HIGL	583-591
FOPP	49- 83	HIGR	170-176
MOFT	178-192	RHGR	51- 58
OCLI	392-399		
THAB	79-139	Ivanov, Vsevolod	
THPP	51- 72	SORL	73- 79

Jackson, Helen Hunt

    CACL   268-277(b)

Jacob, Max

    MICF   30- 35

James, George Henry

    CACL   53- 64(b)

James, Henry

    AMEI   50- 66

    AMFH   279-304

    AMHU   186-208

    AMNE   47- 60

    AMNO   163-189

    AMRE   292-305

    ARNO   172-183

    ASPN   218-234

    BRVL   315-342

    CAAN   145-165

    CEOW   233-248(b)

    CHEL   146-155

    COES   267-292

    CYAL   169-183

    DAEC   234-268

    DEAS   194-208

    DENE   112-121

    ENNO   211-228

    ENNO   428-439

    ETAN   79- 98

    EVHO   149-174

    FAOR   46- 80

    FERE   103-126

    GRTR   126-172

    HENR   ix-xc

    HIOM   213-237

    INDR   300-343

    INENO   13- 34

    LASS   95-125

    LIBN   248-254

    LILI   85- 95

    LIOA   688-700

    LITR   231-240

    LIWM   357-362

    MASM   114-139

    MAWH   90- 99

    MIRO   223-236

    MONA   1- 12

    MOWO   96-101

    MYPO   202-208

James, Henry (cont.)

NEYT	102-109
NOME	5- 15
NOVE	224-244
OPSE	104-117
ORUN	70- 77
POSU	233-245
REAP	145-166
REND	274-302
RIAN	702-742
SHLI	217-228
SHRE	854-865
SHSE	307-315
TEAH	93-112
TEAH	187-214
TIPI	3- 24
TRTH	89-132
TRWO	88- 96
TRWO	112-128
TWGA	49- 67
WITS	45- 64
WOEL	93-106
WOEL	124-143
WRWC	76-106

James, William

FERE	162-168
MOWO	102-110
SHRE	867-883

Janin, Jules

ROAG	122-128

Jarrell, Randall

AMPO	37- 52
BABY	13- 25
MODP	150-156
POPR	156-178

Jarry, Alfred

SEWJ	9- 20
THPP	1- 14

Jean Paul see Richter, Johann Paul

Jefferies, Richard

BOML	173-194

Jeffers, Robinson

AMPP	469-477
BPSW	204-212(b)
CACL	208-218(b)

HIAP	398-410		NEWP	137-145
INTE	109-115		Johnson, Lionel	
MOAM	183-203		DAPA	81- 95
POOT	18- 24			
POPO	129-134		Johnson, Samuel	
			BEJA	226-233
Jefferson, Thomas			CLCO	244-249
COOC	104-110		CRAL	248-260
MACA	342-356 v.1		ESFD	491-508
			HICR	477-496
Jeffrey, Francis			HIEL	226-233
HIMW	111-120		HIMC	79-104
RIFM	2- 9		IMSC	57- 75
			LIHE	989-1004
Jellicoe, Ann			LIHIB	989-1004
ANTH	65- 71		LISH	320-333
			OBCO	80- 96
Jerome, Jerome K.			OPPO	184-222
LINL	238-244		SHSE	190-202
Jewett, Sarah Orne			Johnson, Uwe	
AMFH	324-330		COEN	100-109
PICA	6- 19			
			Jones, David	
Jiménez, Juan Ramón			HERT	200-212
MORL	243-248		MOPO	193-222
Joaquin, Nick				

Jones, Henry Arthur			TRTH	213–232
RIFW	35– 51			
		Joubert, Joseph		
Jones, Idwal			HICT	117–126
CACL	243–256(b)			
		Joyce, James		
Jones, James			APTC	9– 50
AMMO	225–238		ARNO	301–319
COAN	107–112		AXCA	191–236
CRPR	195–206		CAEN	512–521
WWTS	230–250		CHEL	177–187
			CLCO	81– 86
Jones, LeRoi			CLCO	182–189
BLAW	22– 28		CLGR	96– 109
BLAWP	205–214		DOPY	447–477
NASO	190–199		ELFI	66– 77
			ENNO	263–276
Jonson, Ben			ENNO	463–473
CRAL	176–182		FLJB	30– 66
CRAL	217–223		IMSC	316–323
HICR	197–209		INENO	135–151
LIHE	558–563		INLA	23– 47
LIHIA	558–563		INLI	77– 89
LISH	174–181		LILI	106–117
MADR	238–247		LINO	259–275
SHEL	331–336			

Joyce, James (cont.)

LISY	224–229
MAMF	122–132
META	134–140
MIRO	295–312
MOBF	308–375
MOWO	30– 37
NOMW	63–137
NOVE	245–261
OJBO	51– 60
ORUN	62– 69
PRAB	93–103
POOT	278–283
PRVM	27– 40
PRVM	48– 55
PSLP	118–162
VAHE	170–204
WIFT	17– 28
WITS	89–109
WOBO	243–271

Justice, Donald

ALWA	247–257

Juvenal (Decimus Junius Juvenalis)

JUPE	xi–xxi(b)
JUPE	xlviii–lxxvi
LIHRS	477–498

Kafka, Franz

APTC	182–217
ARDO	88– 97
CLCO	383–392
DIMN	37– 67
GENO	215–257
ILLU	29– 34
ILLU	111–148
INLI	257–268
KICA	49– 54
LASI	118–126
LASS	38– 54
LASS	183–195
LINO	160–188
NELI	15– 34
NENA	1– 54
PRVM	83–109
SPLE	254–263
STCL	19– 25
STCL	38– 46
STCL	137–155

Kant, Immanuel

   HIMC   227-232

   LASA   436-452

Kantor, MacKinlay

   PUPN   175-180

Kaplan, Chaim A.

   REHV   186-191

Kasack, Hermann

   GEML   39- 59

Kaufman, George

   AMDR   136-152

   MOAP   154-167(b)

Kazantzakis, Nikos

   INLI   268-298

   ODYS   ix-xxxvi

Keats, John

   ESFD   261-280

   HIEL   320-328

   INLA   99-113

   LIHE   1241-1251

   LIHIC   1241-1251

   OPRI   306-328

   OPSE   3- 49

   POEX   173-199

   POPO   236-243

   WEWU   151-166

   WIHO   283-302

Keller, Gottfried

   GENO   30- 51

Kelly, George

   AMDR   60- 72

Kemler, Edgar

   BIBM   28- 33

Kempton, Murray

   NOIT   161-167

Kennan, George F.

   BIBM   500-514

Kennedy, John Pendleton

   MACA   46- 56 v.2

   RIAN   258-270

Kerouac, Jack

   COAN   120-133

CRPR 206-212

LIRE 101-106

MAMF 148-154

Kesey, Ken

REVA 179-185

King, Clarence

CACL 128-140(b)

King, Martin Luther, Jr.

COPT 197-209

Kingsley, Charles

CAEN 260-267

VILI 18- 36

Kinnell, Galway

ALWA 258-271

Kipling, Rudyard

BRVL 145-154

CAEN 399-405

COEB 184-197

IMSC 324-337

LILI 122-130

LINL 175-182

OPPO 265-294

POOT 28- 38

SELE 232-250

SHSE 329-346

WOBO 105-181

Kizer, Carolyn

ALWA 272-280

Kleist, Heinrich von

COSG 101-139

DETR 216-228

ESTD 202-240

HIGE 215-223

Knight, Eric see
Hallas, Richard

Knowles, John

NEYT 367-373

Koch, Kenneth

ALWA 281-291

Koestler, Arthur

COEC 234-244

LASS 126-133

LILI 130-135

Kops, Bernard

    ANTH   123-129

Krim, Seymour

    REHV   28- 36

Krishnamurti

    BOML   150-159

Kunen, James Simon

    REHV   291-297

Kunitz, Stanley

    COAP   32- 47

    POPR   38- 58

Kuprin, Alexander
    Ivanovich

    ESRN   278-284

Kuttner, Henry

    SETO   311-317

    SETO   319-334

Laclos, Pierre Ambroise
    François Choderlos de

    POSU   108-126

Lacretelle, Jacques de

FRPC   224-251

La Fayette, Marie
    Madelaine

    LINO   108-135

    STHT   131-138

Lagerkvist, Pär Fabian

    GESC   428-435

    SHGO   171-184

Lamartine, Alphonse de

    FRLI   110-121

Lamb, Charles

    HICT   236-246

Lamennais, Félicité-
    Robert de

    FRLI   227-233

Landor, Walter Savage

    LIHE   1162-1167

    LIHIC   1162-1167

Lang, Andrew

    RIFM   132-139

84

Langland, William

    ENEI   151-171

    SHEL   131-138

Lanier, Sidney

    PAGO   450-466

    PAGO   519-522

    TIMW   367-376

Lanson, Gustave

    HIOM   71- 79

Larbaud, Valery

    FRLH   193-208

Lardner, Ring

    FSFH   105-154

    WRIC   1- 36

Larkin, Philip

    MODP   101-110

La Rochefoucauld,
   Francois de

    POSU   22- 28

Larsen, Nella

    NEVA   141-146

Laski, Harold J.

    BIBM   78-100

Lautréamont, Comte de

    CLGR   64- 73

Lawrence, David Herbert

    APTC   51- 78

    ARNO   352-361

    CAEN   494-504

    CEOW   14- 28

    CEOW   421-425

    CHEL   189-198

    CONT   105-113

    CONTI   124-137

    DAEC   103-120

    ENLT   209-228

    ENNO   245-261

    ENNO   454-462

    EVRR   141-153

    IMSC   338-343

    INENO   111-134

    LASS   293-306

    LILI   144-164

    LINL   182-189

    MIRO   270-279

Lawrence, David Herbert (cont.)		Le Fanu, Joseph Sheridan	
MOBF	225-307	LINL	122-127
MOPE	285-300		
MOPR	160-168	Legaré, Hugh Swinton	
NOMW	139-186	MACA	114-124 v.2
NOVE	208-223	Lehmann, Wilhelm	
POOT	86 -91	GEML	19- 35
TEAH	221-228		
WITS	110-133	Leiber, Fritz, Jr.	
WOEL	40- 49	SETO	283-302
WOWE	107-161	Leinster, Murray	
		SETO	47- 65
Lawrence, Thomas Edward			
DENE	294-326	Leiris, Michel	
LILI	164-170	AGIN	61- 68
LINL	288-293	NELI	61- 73
Lawson, John Howard		Leivick, H.	
AMDR	256-262	YILI	348-381
Leavis, F. R.		Leland, C. G.	
BEYC	145-177	TIMW	41- 49
LASI	221-238		
LASS	289-297	Lely, Gilbert	
LILI	170-180	BIBM	159-176
RIFM	269-284		

Leonard, Daniel

   LIHA   358-368

   MACA   207-213 v.1

Leonov, Leonid

   CLCO   250-256

   HISL   175-190

   SORL   193-207

Leopardi, Giacomo

   HIIL   399-410

   HIMW   272-278

   SEPR   11-184

Lermontov, Mikhail
   Yurievich

   OURL   46- 56

   RUNO   50- 63

Leskov, Nikolai

   ILLU   83-109

   LINL   420-426

   RUNO   214-235

Lessing, Doris

   POBF   65- 86

Lessing, Gotthold Ephraim

   ESTD   189-201

   HICT   33- 48

   HIGE   143-150

   HIMC   151-175

   MADR   318-323

Lever, Charles

   CAEN   187-192

Leverson, Ada

   LINL   263-269

Levertov, Denise

   ALWA   292-305

   COAP   175-196

Levin, Meyer

   NOIT   209-228

Lévi-Strauss, Claude

   AGIN   70- 81

   LASI   239-250

Lewis, Alun

   MODP   141-150

Lewis, C. S.

   LILI   204-212

Lewis, Matthew Gregory

 BEJA   265-271

Lewis, Meriwether

 BOTC   14- 25

 FRWE   11- 38

 MASM   213-220

Lewis, Sinclair

 AFGT   92-102

 AMBL   92- 98

 AMDA   94-105

 AMFH   660-668

 AMMO   107-118

 AMNF   166-179

 AMNO   302-314

 ARNO   293-300

 CAAN   354-367

 COYE   497-506

 FIYA   89-106

 LAPR   69-150

 MACA   360-369 v.3

 MASM   171-179

 MONA   121-126

 NOAM   9- 44

 PUPN   58- 67

 ROAL   323-328

 SEMA   46- 80

 TWEN   408-415

 WOWE   164-194

Lewis, Wyndham

 INLA   83- 94

 LILI   213-222

Liben, Meyer

 REHV   229-236

Lieber, Francis

 MACA   93- 98 v.2

Lincoln, Abraham

 MACA   152-160 v.2

Lindsay, Howard

 MOAP   140-150(b)

Lindsay, Vachel

 COYE   409-422

 HIAP   233-242

Linnaeus, Carl

 BINA   27- 43

Lippard, George

    RIAN   319-326

Livings, Henry

    ANTH   129-135

Livy

    HILL   227-232

    LIHRO   464-482

Lizardi, José Joaquín

    CEOW   357-387(b)

Llosa, Mario Vargas see
    Vargas Llosa, Mario

Lodge, George Cabot
    (1873-1907)

    SHRE   749-852(b)

Lodge, Thomas

    IDAE   80- 93

Logan, John

    ALWA   306-317

London, Jack

    AMNF   133-143

    CAAN   222-229

    CACL   185-195(b)

    COED   23- 29

    COYE   222-231

    DEAS   347-353

    RANU   38- 46

    REAN   139-216

    RORH   108-118(b)

Longfellow, Henry Wadsworth

    AMPP   42- 53

    AMSL   152-157

    BIBM   551-560

    COOC   265-276

    DIVC   7- 43(b)
                   v.10

    FLNE   153-177

    LIOA   322-346

    LITR   128-133

    MASM   160-170

    NEYT   86- 92

    RIAN   309-318

    ROAL   180-187

    SHRE   98-104

Longinus			LIOA	374-383
ESFD	471-490		LIOA	408-421
HICL	152-174		LIOA	447-457
LISH	97-110		LITR	160-166
			MACA	460-472 v. 2
Longstreet, Augustus Baldwin			ROAL	193-199
MACA	166-172 v. 2			

Lorca, Féderico García see
   García Lorca, Féderico

Lowell, Robert

			AMLI	57- 76
Lovecraft, H. P.			AMPO	17- 36
EXIN	243-260		AMPP	577-585
			COAP	134-159
Lovelace, Richard			COCH	150-157
LICR	397-405		MOAM	321-350
MASM	67- 76		MODP	32- 41
			MODP	188-193
Lowell, Amy			MOPE	256-263
HIAP	182-191		MOPO	223-251
			MOPR	226-238
Lowell, James Russell			OCLI	404-418
AMPP	59- 69		PLDO	324-330
AMSL	168-174		POPR	24- 37
COOC	292-301		WWSS	335-368
COPW	ix-xvii(b)			
FLNE	321-332			
HIOM	200-206			

Lucan (Marcus Annaeus
   Lucanus)

   ENEI   94- 99

   LERBL   451-457

   LIHRS   238-263

   POPO   272-277

Lucian

   HICL   146-152

   SEWO   vii-xxxi

Lucilius, Gaius

   LIHRO   171-178

Lucretius

   CLRE   85- 90

   HILL   69- 76

   LIHRO   202-221

Lugones, Leopoldo

   SPAL   272-277

Lukács, Georg

   AGIN   82- 92

   LASI   325-347

Lummis, Charles F.

   CACL   292-303(b)

Luther, Martin

   HIGE   97-102

Lyly, John

   IDAE   109-121

Lynd, Robert S.

   BOTC   216-228

Macaulay, Rose

   LILI   247-252

Macaulay, Thomas Babington

   HICT   489-495

   HIOC   125-131

   POPO   198-204

   VILI   1- 12

McAuley, James

   ESPO   177-195

McCarthy, Mary

   COAN   54- 64

   CRPR   239-255

   FIFO   128-135

   PICA   170-186

   WWSS   283-316

McCoy, Horace

    TOGW   137-162

McCullers, Carson

    COAN   48- 53

    CRPR   84- 94

    FIFO   243-258

    PICA   161-169

    RAIS   205-229

    WOWE   275-285

Macdonald, Ross

    AFTE   147-159

McGinley, Phyllis

    FAAH   71- 78

Machajski, Waclaw

    BIBM   486-496

Machiavelli, Niccolò

    HIIL   208-222

    MAEN   89-107

McKay, Claude

    BLAWP   54- 63

    NENO   67- 75

    NEVA   163-168

MacKaye, Percy

    HIAD   27- 45 v.2

Mackenzie, Henry

    BEJA   197-203

MacLeish, Archibald

    AMDS   184-190

    AMPL   119-125

    AMPP   486-492

    CLCO   3- 9

    HIAP   448-457

McLuhan, Marshall

    CONR   22- 28

    LASA   410-418

    LASI   251-257

Maeterlinck, Maurice

    OCOR   165-178

Mahan, Alfred T.

    BOTC   110-121

Mahfouz, Nagib

    FISL   66- 72

Mailer, Norman

AFTE	193-231
AMDA	197-203
AMMO	171-179
COAN	112-119
CONR	81-153
CRPR	143-171
ETAN	198-209
FIFO	33- 38
LASS	409-421
LIRE	175-188
MAMF	154-162
MYPO	234-243
NENA	108-140
OCLI	422-436
RAIS	140-151
WWTS	251-278

Malamud, Bernard

AFTR	116-130
COAN	65- 79
CONT	202-207
CONTI	216-222
CRPR	218-224
KICA	156-163

LANI	102-122
LASS	280-288
NENA	168-178
OCLI	437-446
RAIS	161-168
REHV	71- 86

Malcolm X

AMLI	409-419
NASO	149-172

Mallarmé, Stéphane

AXCA	16- 28
CLGR	7- 14
CRCO	149-156
DIPA	265-276
GUCF	226-239
HIOM	452-463
LASA	322-329
LIOS	127-321
SYPO	320-328

Malory, Sir Thomas

IDAE	19- 25

Malraux, André

    BIBM   137-150

    FRPC   279-298

    LICA   175-214

    PISA   275-295

    SHLI   566-574

    TRWO   170-183

    WITS   192-200

Manifold, John

    ESPO   61- 69

Manly, William L.

    CACL   31- 43(b)

Mann, Horace

    BOTC   57- 68

Mann, Thomas

    COSG   241-262

    DIMN   68- 98

    GENO   76- 98

    GENO   258-296

    HACR   71- 87

    IMTR   164-241

    INLI   219-256

    KICA   97-107

    LASI   269-279

    THBU   314-320

    TIPI   25- 42

    WITS   213-247

Mansfield, Katherine

    CEOW   47- 52

    LILI   278-283

Manzoni, Alessandro

    HIIL   389-398

    MAEN   192-227

    MOIN   8- 18

Marcus Aurelius

    ECGR   168-175

Marechal, Leopoldo

    INMA   17- 22

Marlowe, Christopher

    LIHE   508-518

    LIHIA   508-518

    MADR   191-211

    SPTR   149-165

Marquand, John Phillip

AMFI 253-270

AMMO 151-164

CAAN 438-443

CONT 122-130

FIYA 107-134

Márquez, García see
García Márquez, Gabriel

Marquis, Donald Robert
Perry

FAAH 61- 70

Marryat, Frederick

COES 173-180

FAOR 276-285

Marshall, John

MACA 20- 27 v.2

Martial (Marcus Valerius
Martialis)

HICL 256-268

LIHRS 397-421

Martin du Gard, Roger

DENE 43- 53

FRLH 245-252

LYCE 254-287

Martínez Sierra, Gregorio

MAMS 276-288

Marvell, Andrew

POEX 82- 88

Marx, Karl

TRTH 197-212

LASI 305-324

Mascola, Dionys

NELI 195-211

Masefield, John

ENLT 294-305

LILI 287-293

Masters, Edgar Lee

COAM 146-153

HIAP 226-232

Mather, Cotton

CEOW 13- 51(b)

MACA 106-117 v.1

Matson, Norman

ASPN 166-171

Maugham, W. Somerset

    AMBL   226-231

    ARNO   268-276

    IMTR   59- 85

    INLI   102-112

    LILI   297-304

    RIFW   92-109

Maupassant, Guy de

    ELFI   50- 55

Mauriac, François

    FRPC   142-172

    GUCF   140-164

    MARE   vii-xx

    WWFS   37- 49

May, Thomas

    ENEI   415-421

Mayakovsky, Vladimir V.

    HISL   53- 68

    SORL   19- 31

Mayer, Hans

    LASI   348-355

Mayhew, Jonathan

    LIHA   121-140

Mazzini, Giuseppe

    HIIL   421-428

Medici, Lorenzo de'

    HIIL   136-147

Mela, Pomponius

    LIHRS   101-106

Melville, Herman

    AMDA   76- 86

    AMFH   149-157

    AMHU   154-160

    AMNF   25- 34

    AMNO   84-102

    AMPP   227-235

    AMRE   371-514

    ARFI   188-213

    ARNO   130-135

    ASPN   199-206

    CAAN   58- 81

    COCH   76-99

    CONT   29- 40

    COOC   220-231

    CYAL   91- 99

    ETAN   34- 47

Melville, Herman (cont.)

EVHO	113-140
FRAL	232-326
FRAL	375-396
INDR	200-233
LIRE	48- 59
LISY	21- 26
LITR	169-182
LODA	403-408
LODA	429-437
LODA	520-552
LYCE	288-294
MACA	258-267 v.2
POBL	165-237
PSLP	66-117
REAP	91-112
RIAN	363-411
RIFA	375-385
ROAL	149-158
SEES	184-198
SHRE	1031-1061
STCA	131-161
TEAH	67- 77
TIMW	145-179
TIMW	250-259

TRWO	36- 76
TWGA	19- 33
VILA	82- 87

Menander

ANCR	199-204
ECGR	141-154
HIGL	643-662

Mencken, Henry Lewis

AFGT	83- 91
BIBM	28- 33
BOTC	197-206
COYE	449-468
LAPR	3- 66
OBCO	203-212

Mendelé, Mokher Sefarim

MATM	7- 14
YILI	39- 60

Meredith, George

AGFI	205-251
ARNO	152-163
BRVL	299-314
CAEN	336-351

COES	173-180	AMPO	107-123
CORE	245-256 v.2	POPR	179-204
ENNO	183-194		
ENNO	409-418	Michaux, Henri	
LIHE	1455-1463	COFP	155-160
LIHIC	1455-1463	NELI	119-132
LINL	109-121	SEWR	vii-xxi
REND	215-230	Michelangelo see	
VIDE	322-327	Buonarroti, Michelangelo	
WOVN	279-298	Mill, John Stuart	
WOVN	371-380	RIFM	37- 45

Meredith, William

ALWA 318-326

Mérimée, Prosper

LASI 261-268

LINL 347-353

Merrill, James

ALWA 327-348

Merritt, A.

EXIN 189-207

Merwin, W. S.

ALWA 349-381

Millay, Edna St. Vincent

HIAP 265-274

SHLI 681-687

SHLI 744-793(b)

Miller, Arthur

AMDA 165-174

AMDS 3- 17

AMPL 35- 52

COTH 293-303

LASS 385-391

MOAP 247-263

MYPO 225-233

Miller, Arthur (cont.)

OCLI	49- 55
WWTS	197-230

Miller, Henry

AMDA	136-148
BPSW	213-218(b)
COEA	493-502
INDI	313-338
INTE	37- 72
LASS	88- 94
LISI	38- 44(b)
LISI	45-109
LISI	209-214
NELI	51- 59
REHV	22- 32
WRIR	128-145
WWSS	165-192

Miller, J. Hillis

CRCO	195-217

Miller, Joaquin

HIAP	45- 50
RORH	54- 62(b)
TIMW	311-318

Miller, Vassar

POOP	114-132

Milton, John

AMRE	306-312
CHEL	89-100
ENEI	430-447
HIEL	133-139
LERBL	471-476
LICR	106-121
LIHE	673-696
LIHIA	673-696
OPPO	156-183
SHEL	392-402
TILI	276-296
WEWU	50- 66
WIHO	190-204

Minturno, Antonio
Sebastiano

HICR	51- 57

Mirbeau, Octave

CLCO	471-485

Miró, Gabriel

LAPO	159-197

Mistral, Gabriela

    SEPO   9- 16(b)

Mitchell, Weir

    AMFH   305-322

Mofolo, Thomas

    SEST   39- 50

Molière, Jean-Baptiste
  Poquelin

    DIPA   247-264

    EVPP   63- 72

    HIWL   184-189

    MADR   286-300

    ONAC   1- 11

    ONAC   165-173(b)

    STHT   97-104

    WOMM   Pref. (b)

    WOMM   1- 70(b)

Monroe, Harriet

    HIAP   141-149

    RORH   147-156(b)

Montaigne, Michel
  Eyquem de

    COESA   18- 26

    CORE   87-100 v.1

    STHT   39- 49

    TILI   209-220

Montale, Eugenio

    GUCI   177-187

    SEPM   ix-xxiv

Montherlant, Henry de

    DIPA   89-109

    FRLH   209-219

    LINL   365-375

    MOFT   93-111

Moody, William Vaughn

    HIAD   7- 17 v.2

Moore, C. L.

    SETO   303-318

Moore, George

    CAEN   411-416

    LIHE   1493-1498

    LIHIC   1493-1498

    LILI   330-337

    REND   262-273

    TILI   472-477

Moore, Marianne		More, Thomas	
BABY	156-164	CLRE	154-159
DAEC	141-171		
HIAP	320-325	Moreau, Gustave	
MOAM	204-221	ROAG	289-299
MODP	125-133	Moretti, Marino	
MOMP	41- 48	MOIN	202-209
MOPE	201-218		
MOPO	103-118	Mörike, Eduard Friedrich	
MOPR	140-146	ERGO	163-177
ORUN	42- 50	Morley, Christopher Darlington	
PLDO	121-155	FAAH	79- 88
POAG	162-187		
POOP	8- 16	Morley, John	
WWSS	61- 88	RIFM	99-112
Moravia, Alberto		Morris, Charles	
GUCI	29- 56	ESFD	77- 92
OCLI	447-467	ESFD	97-103
PISA	36- 56		
WWFS	209-229	Morris, William	
		DROR	209-230
More, Paul Elmer		LIHE	1430-1438
COYE	383-391	LIHIC	1430-1438
TRTH	3- 14	SELE	219-231

VIDE 248-253

Morris, Wright

AFTE 11- 27

FIFO 328-341

LANI 152-169

Morrison, Arthur

LINL 206-212

Mortimer, John

ANTH 214-226

Moss, Howard

ALWA 382-395

Motley, John Lothrop

FLNE 344-352

Mowatt, Anna C. O.

HIAM 310-319

Muir, Edwin

MODP 42- 49

Muir, John

CACL 142-149(b)

TIMW 418-428

Mulholland, John

CLCO 147-152

Müller, Adam

HIMW 291-297

Munk, Kaj

FIPL 9- 21

Murdoch, Iris

CONE 260-265

FABU 106-132

LUGD 181-212

POBF 178-195

Murfree, Mary Noailles

RIAN 592-598

Murger, Henri

LINL 341-347

Murry, John Middleton

LILI 356-362

Musil, Robert

LINL 445-457

ORUN 203-210

Myrdal, Gunnar

   BOTC   239-250

Nabokov, Vladimir

   ASPR   318-327

   CRPR   63- 78

   KICA   117-141

   OCLI   473-485

   STCL   94-101

   STCL   138-155

   WROW   15- 34

Naevius, Gnaeus

   LIHRO   93-100

Nash, Ogden

   FAAH   89- 98

Nashe, Thomas

   IDAE   210-237

Nathan, Robert

   CAAN   339-405

Neal, John

   RIAN   165-177

Nekrasov, Victor

   HISL   306-316

Nemerov, Howard

   BABY   35- 41

   MOPR   255-261

   POOP   239-250

   POPR   116-133

Neruda, Pablo

   HEMP   vii-xix

   NEDE   ix-xlvi

   TWPO   7- 17

Nerval, Gérard de

   CLGR   58- 63

   GEDN   7- 30

Newman, Cardinal

   BRVL   380-406

Nicolson, Harold

   CLCO   121-127

Nietzsche, Friedrich

   COSG   203-235

   HICT   581-586

   HIOM   336-356

LAES	141-177	LIES	122-131
LISH	562-567		
MALR	168-185	Norton, Charles Eliot	
OJBO	42- 50	FLNE	463-469
SPTR	253-259	Nossack, Hans Erich	
		GEML	63- 85
Nomad, Max			
BIBM	485-499	Novalis, Friedrich von Hardenburg	
Nordhoff, Walter		COSG	66-100
CACL	17- 30(b)	HIMW	82- 88
Norris, Frank		Noyes, Alfred	
AMEI	250-274	LILI	379-384
AMFH	624-630		
AMNF	97-105	O'Brien, Fitz-James	
CAAN	216-222	EXIN	62- 72
CACL	175-183(b)	O'Casey, Sean	
COYE	211-221	COTH	169-191
ETAN	105-115	ENLT	114-121
LIOA	749-754	LILI	385-392
MACA	329-334 v.3	MADR	566-571
MAWH	124-135		
REAN	3- 66	O'Connor, Edwin	
		PUPN	197-203
North, Christopher			

O'Connor, Flannery

    MIAN   99-117

    REHV   171-177

    SHGO   117-138

    STCL   78- 83

O'Connor, Frank

    LANI   87-100

    WWFS   161-182

Odell, Jonathan

    LIHAR   98-129

Odets, Clifford

    AMDR   263-277

    MOAP   186-201

O'Flaherty, Liam

    NOFI   65- 90

Ogden, Schubert M.

    COPT   71- 76

O'Hara, Frank

    ALWA   396-412

O'Hara, John

    CONT   161-168

    TOGW   129-136

Olesha, Yury

    HISL   162-174

    RUNO   346-355

    SORL   118-125

Ollier, Claude

    NEFN   99-105

Olmsted, Frederick Law

    PAGO   219-231

Olson, Charles

    AMPO   136-145

Omar Khayyám

    RUOK   49- 57(b)

O'Neill, Eugene

    AFGT   103-113

    AMBL   119-127

    AMDA   158-164

    AMDR   77-120

    AMPL   15- 34

    AWTC   103-109

    COYE   534-548

CYAL	249-254	LASS	331-339
FIMA	301-322	LILI	403-408
FRSS	62- 68	OPSE	151-172
HIAD	165-206 v. 2	WROW	153-171
INLI	49- 64		
LIOA	928-934		
MADR	640-661		
MOAP	50- 77		
MOPW	282-328		
ORUN	151-160		
READ	39- 70		
ROAL	363-368		

Osborne, John

ANTH   39- 57

LILI   409-414

MOBD   48- 57

THPP   222-234

Otis, James

LIHA   30- 52

Onetti, Juan Carlos

INMA   173-205

Otway, Thomas

REDR   139-149

Opatoshu, Joseph

YILI   326-347

Ovechkin, Valentin

HISL   295-305

Opitz, Martin

MERS   22- 34

Ovid

HILL   201-226

LACL   85- 98

LIHRO   422-445

POPO   264-270

Orwell, George

COEA   543-551(b)

CONE   148-166

Owen, Alun

DENE   269-279

ANTH   183-202

Owen, Wilfred

    HERT   121-135

    LILI   414-419

Page, Thomas Nelson

    AMFH   357-362

    PAGO   604-616

Paine, Robert Treat, Jr.

    MACA   288-295 v.2

Paine, Thomas

    BEDA   10- 23

    BOTC   1- 13

    COOC   98-104

    LIHA   452-474

    LIHAR   35- 49

    MACA   327-341 v.1

Painter, George

    MOWO   143-160

Panova, Vera Fedorovna

    HISL   272-283

Panzini, Alfredo

    MOIN   126-137

Parain, Brice

    LYCE   228-241

Pareto, Vilfredo

    SPLE   291-321

Parker, Dorothy

    FAAH   99-108

    WWFS   69- 82

Parker, Theodore

    MACA   414-425 v.2

Parkman, Francis

    FRWE   69- 81

Parrington, V. L.

    INDR   557-563

Partridge, Eric

    BIBM   131-136

Pascal, Blaise

    CLGR   44- 51

    PRTR   148-171

    SPLE   103-128

    STHT   74- 95

Pasternak, Boris Leonidovich

    BIBM   420-472

    HISL   150-161

    INLI   305-321

    MOWO   136-142

    OCLI   486-497

    RUNO   360-378

    RUTH   250-263

    SORL   218-230

    VOSN   183-212(b)

    WWSS   111-136

Pater, Walter Horatio

    BRVL   457-476

    DAPA   36- 52

    HICT   544-551

    HIOM   381-399

    PSLP   163-218

    WOVN   381-404

Patrizzi, Francesco

    HICR   94-102

Paulding, James Kirke

    MACA   212-221 v. 2

    RIAN   185-200

Paustovsky, Konstantin

    HISL   260-271

Pavese, Cesare

    NOIT   135-150

Payne, John Howard

    HIAM   163-187

Peabody, Josephine Preston

    HIAD   17- 23 v. 2

Peacock, Thomas Love

    CAEN   207-212

    DROR   115-121

Péguy, Charles Pierre

    BAVE   13- 41(b)

    COMF   55- 79

Péladan, Joseph

    ROAG   316-325

Perelman, S. J.

    WWSS   241-256

Peretz, Itzhak Leib

    MATM   25- 42

Peretz, Itzhak Leib (cont.)

   NOIT   93- 98

   YILI   99-133

Pérez Galdós, Benito

   DOPE   7- 30

Perse, St.-John

   GUCF   245-257

   LIOS   365-419

   MICF   94- 99

   SPLE   222-251

Persius (Aulus Persius
   Flaccus)

   HICL   248-253

   JUPE   xxi-xxxii(b)

   LIHRS   224-236

Petrarch

   ENEI   185-192

   HIIL   80-100

   WIHO   106-123

Petroni, Guglielmo

   GUCI   127-133

Petronius Arbiter

   LIHRS   138-158

Petry, Ann

   NENO   180-185

Phaedrus

   LIHRS   107-124

Phelps, Elizabeth S. see
   Ward, Elizabeth Stuart
   Phelps

Phillips, Wendell

   MACA   140-147 v.3

Photius

   HICL   175-186

Pilnyak, Boris

   HISL   135-149

   SORL   59- 66

Pindar

   GRWA   85- 103

   HIGL   190-203

   HIGR   58- 63

   LAGL   106-116

   ODPI   v-xii

Pinero, Arthur Wing

  RIFW   52- 80

Pinget, Robert

  FONN   127-132

Pinski, David

  YILI   182-196

Pinter, Harold

  ANTH   233-261

  MOBD   65- 70

  MOBD   122-163

  SEST   57- 74

  THAB   198-217

  THPP   197-211

  WWTS   347-368

Pirandello, Luigi

  COTH   127-143

  HIIL   478-483

  MADR   435-445

  MAMI   49- 61

  MOIN   137-154

  MOPW   230-275

  NAMA   vii-xxvii

  NAMA   363-375

  SPLE   146-170

  TOCN   ix-xviii

Pisarev, Dmitri

  HIOM   254-265

Platen-Hallermünde,
  August von

  ESTD   259-269

Plath, Sylvia

  ALWA   412-422

  LASI   295-302

  MODP   75- 82

Plato

  CLRE   69- 79

  CRAL   3- 22

  ECGR   79- 93

  EVPP   38- 47

  HIGL   505-542

  HIGR   130-146

  LAGL   212-233

  LIFD   219-224

  LISH   5- 20

  LISH   57- 66

Plato (cont.)

RHGR	26- 39
TILI	82- 88
WOPL	xi-xlviii

Plautus, Titus Maccius

HILL	35- 43
LIHRO	117-146

Pliny the Elder (Gaius
Plinius Secundus)

LIHRS	281-310

Pliny the Younger (Gaius
Plinius Caecilius
Secundus)

HICL	270-279
HILL	308-315
LIHRS	425-443

Plotinus

CLGR	15- 22
LISH	112-124

Plutarch

ECGR	181-209
HIGL	137-146
HIGH	819-825

HIGR	252-257

Poe, Edgar Allan

AMFH	77- 96
AMPP	130-146
AMSL	187-196
AXCA	13- 19
COOC	174-192
CYAL	68- 78
DEAS	115-141
ESFD	385-423
EVHO	215-226
EXIN	46- 61
FAOR	172-215
FRAL	132-174
HIOC	152-163
ILLU	172-178
INDR	234-261
INLA	211-220
LIOA	292-307
LIOA	387-397
LITR	105-114
LODA	370-382
LODA	408-415
MUFP	3- 27

111

OPRI	132-150
POBL	100-165
REVA	127-136
RIAN	300-306
RIFA	368-374
ROAL	108-120
SHLI	179-190
SHRE	10- 20
SHRE	966-984
SHSE	227-245
STCA	65- 81
TILI	395-403
TOCC	27- 35
WIHO	335-347
WOWI	262-283
WOWI	347-357

Polybius

HIGL	772-777

Pope, Alexander

ENEI	498-509
HICR	452-261
HIEL	452-461
INLA	169-179

LIHE	921-932
LIHIB	921-932
LISH	236-247
POPO	61- 67
SHEL	549-554
WEWU	81-104
WIHO	207-214

Porter, Katherine Anne

IMTR	25- 58
PICA	136-151
REHV	103-121
SEES	136-156
SEST	75- 93
WOWE	264-273
WWSS	137-164

Post, Emily

CLCO	372-382

Potter, Stephen

BIBM	473-478

Poulet, Georges

CRCO	74-135

Pound, Ezra

AMPP	389-408
CEOW	40- 46
CONT	113-118
COYE	510-521
COYE	558-573
DAEC	30- 67
ESFD	364-371
EXRE	119-124
FIMA	323-344
HIAP	163-181
INDI	61- 85
INDR	493-501
INLA	75- 81
INLI	67- 76
MASM	302-323
MAWH	178-190
MOAM	155-181
MOMP	18- 34
MOPE	35- 53
MOPE	447-472
MOPO	29- 43
MOPR	49- 74
ORUN	291-311

PLDO	273-285
POMI	147-153
POOT	119-145
SEST	118-129
TOCC	162-182
TWEN	55- 66
WAFE	184-190
WWSS	35- 60

Powell, Anthony

CONE	238-244
LILI	440-446
LINL	294-303

Powell, Dawn

BIBM	526-533

Powers, J. F.

SHGO	91-115
KICA	149-155

Pratolini, Vasco

GUCI	57- 86

Praz, Mario

BIBM	151-157
BIBM	653-668

Prescott, William Hickling

    FLNE   337-343

    LIOA   525-530

Prévost, d'Exiles
   Antoine François

    STHT   149-157

Price, Reynolds

    AFTE   107-123

Priestley, J. B.

    LILI   455-460

Prior, Matthew

    LIHE   908-914

    LIHIB   908-914

Prishvin, Mikhail

    HISL   191-202

    SORL   105-111

Propertius, Sextus

    HILL   194-200

    LIHRO   410-422

Protagoras

    HIGL   342-347

Proust, Marcel

    AXCA   132-190

    CLGR   96-109

    FRLH   3- 46

    FRPC   1- 29

    ILLU   201-217

    INLI   113-137

    KICA   108-116

    LINO   189-225

    MIRO   280-294

    MORL   363-371

    MOWO   143-160

    STHT   291-321

    TILI   453-471

    WITS   183-191

Purcell, Victor

    BIBM   364-402

Purdy, James

    AMSS   90- 98

    COAN   143-149

    OCLI   498-505

Pushkin, Alexander Sergeyevich

    EUON   388-441(b)

Pushkin, Alexander
  Sergeyevich (cont.)

  OURL   32- 45

  POPP   13- 48(b)

  POSU   160-180

  RUNO   14- 50

  TRTH   31- 59

Pynchon, Thomas

  TRWO   228-234

Quasimodo, Salvatore

  GUCI   187-200

Quevedo y Villegas,
  Francisco Gómez de

  OTIN   36- 42

Quintilian

  HICL   289-321

  LIHRS   311-337

Raabe, Wilhelm

  GENO   143-177

Rabelais, François

  FIBG   xxi-xxxi

  TILI   162-178

Rabinowitz, Shalon Nahum see
  Aleichem, Sholom

Racine, Jean

  BEPR   3- 10

  BEPR   101-107

  BEPR   208-219

  BEPR   303-319

  CLGR   51- 57

  DETR   75-105

  HIWL   190-195

  MADR   273-281

  META   11- 38

  PRTR   100-106

  SPTR   224-238

  STHT   117-130

Radcliffe, Ann (Ward)

  BEJA   247-265

  CAEN   117-122

  REND   90- 96

Radiguet, Raymond

  GUCF   122-128

Ransom, John Crowe

  AMPP   530-540

HIAP	362-372	Rechy, John	
INDR	502-555	CONR	53- 61
MOMP	49- 62		
MOPE	120-127	Reed, John	
MOPO	81-102	COYE	472-478
ORUN	174-179	Reisen, Abraham	
POAG	87-100	YILI	198-220
POOT	204-209		
		Renan, Ernest	
Rascoe, Burton		FRLI	314-320
EVPP	120-126		
		Renault, Mary	
Rattigan, Terence		AFTE	81- 87
RIFW	148-160		
		Rice, Elmer	
Rawicz, Piotr		AMDR	229-239
REHV	178-185	MOAP	8- 21
Raymond, Marcel		Rich, Adrienne	
CRCO	21- 48	ALWA	423-441
Read, Herbert		Richard, Jean-Pierre	
ESFD	372-382	CRCO	141-164
LILIC	12- 18		
		Richards, I. A.	
Reade, Charles		ESFD	97-105
CAEN	243-251	IMSC	349-377

Richards, I.A. (cont.)

    LILIC   22- 28

    LISH   613-627

    LISH   641-646

Richardson, Dorothy

    ARNO   320-328

    CAEN   505-512

    LILIC   28- 33

Richardson, Jack

    THPP   284-290

Richardson, Samuel

    ARNO   46- 51

    BEJA   53- 87

    CAEN   46- 57

    ENNO   45- 63

    ENNO   307-322

    INEN   63- 71

    LIES   26- 49

    LINL   11- 20

    LODA   29- 42

    NOVE   39- 58

    REND   23- 41

    RINO   135-238

ROAG   95-100

Richter, Johann Paul

    HIMW   100-109

Riding, Laura

    MOMP   103-113

Riley, James Whitcomb

    FAAH   109-116

    HIAP   59- 66

Rilke, Rainer Maria

    DIMN   3- 36

    PONN   9- 54

Rimbaud, Jean Nicholas Arthur

    AXCA   269-283

    CLGR   128-138

    CLRE   268-274

    GUCF   229-235

    LIOS   89-126

    MORL   389-394

    POEX   149-172

    RICO   1- 6

    SEHE   vii-xx(b)

Robbe-Grillet, Alain

    EXNO   9- 19

    LINO   275-299

    NEFN   113-123

    NELI   225-234

    OCLI   511-519

Roberts, Elizabeth Maddox

    CAAN   389-396

    PICA   123-135

Robertson, T. W.

    RIFW   19- 31

Robinson, Edwin Arlington

    AFGT   28- 36(b)

    AMBL   13- 19

    AMEI   325-333

    AMPP   262-292

    BABY   209-230

    COCH   129-143

    ESFD   341-347

    FERE   268-277

    FIMA   345-367

    HIAP   107-132

    MOAM   40- 59

    MOPR   104-110

    ROAL   269-275

Robinson, Henry Morton

    CLCO   182-189

Roethke, Theodore

    AMPP   564-577

    BABY   147-152

    COAP   48- 71

    COCH   216-245

    LASA   254-281

    MOAM   301-319

    OCLI   520-526

    POMI   162-182

    POPR   3- 23

Rölvaag, Ole

    COYE   76- 82

    MACA   387-396 v. 3

Romains, Jules

    FRLH   221-244

    FRPC   252-278

Ronsard, Pierre de

    HICR   119-126

Roosevelt, Theodore
  BIBM   63- 77

Rosenberg, Isaac
  HERT   109-121
  MASM   281-301

Rosenfeld, Isaac
  REHV   3- 21

Rosenfeld, Morris
  YILI   151-164

Rosenfeld, Paul
  CLCO   503-519

Rossetti, Christina
  COESB   54- 60
  CORE   257-265 v. 2

Rossetti, Dante Gabriel
  BRVL   174-185
  DAPA   3- 18
  LIHE   1421-1426
  LIHIC   1421-1426

Rostand, Edmond
  OCDR   210-215

Rostand, Jean
  NELI   161-174

Roth, Philip
  BREA   354-366
  REHV   306-328

Rousseau, Jean-Jacques
  LIWM   113-121
  STHT   158-184

Roussel, Raymond
  FONN   78- 87

Rousset, Jean
  CRCO   187-194

Roy, Jules
  LYCE   242-247

Royce, Josiah
  SHRE   884-904

Ruhle, Jurgen
  LASI   357-364

Ruiz, Juan
  BOGL   xiii-lv

Rulfo, Juan

    INMA   246-275

Ruskin, John

    BRVL   345-356

    DROR   195-209

    FLNE   463-468

    HIOC   136-149

    LIHE   1336-1343

    LIHIC   1336-1343

    VIDE   208-216

Russell, Bertrand

    MOWO   111-129

Russell, Eric Frank

    SETO   133-150

Russell, George William

    LILIC   59- 64

Rymer, Thomas

    HICR   391-397

Saba, Umberto

    GUCI   161-167

Sachs, Nelly

OCHI   v-xii

Sade, Marquis de

    BIBM   174-227

    MOWO   56- 70

Sagan, Françoise

    WWFS   301-309

Sainte-Beuve, Charles
    Augustin

    FRLI   248-260

    HICT   301-329

    HIOC   34- 72

Saint-Exupéry, Antoine de

    CLGR   109-113

    FRPC   201-223

    LICA   215-246

Saint-Simon, Claude-Henri
    de Rouvroy de

    FRLI   87- 90

    POSU   29- 54

Saintsbury, George

    CLCO   366-371

    HIOM   416-428

Saintsbury, George (cont.)

    RIFM   139-149

Saki (H. H. Munro)

    LINL   219-224

Salacrou, Armand

    MOFT   112-130

Salinger, Jerome David

    AMMO   195-209

    ASPR   234-239

    COAN   95-105

    CONT   230-240

    CONTI   194-201

    CRPR   25- 62

    LANI   55- 67

    NENA   141-164

    OCLI   537-543

    RAIS   259-289

    REAP   197-229

    WROW   35- 41

Sallust

    HILL   95-100

    LACL   63- 84

Sandburg, Carl

    AFGT   67- 73

    COYE   409-415

    HIAP   242-251

Santayana, George

    HIAP   67- 78

Santos, Bienvenido

    NEWP   125-133

Sappho

    CLRE   41- 46

    HIGL   138-147

Saroyan, William

    AMPL   75- 80

    CLCO   26- 31

    READ   111-119

Sarraute, Nathalie

    AGIN   100-111

    NEFN   125-134

    NELI   235-248

    OCLI   544-554

    WROW   172-188

Sartre, Jean-Paul

AGIN	93- 99
ARDO	6- 23
CLCO	393-403
COMF	34- 45
COMF	127-169
CONTI	180-186
COTH	201-211
DIPA	166-183
FRLH	313-319
FRPC	299-324
FRSS	35- 43
INLI	163-206
LICA	249-284
LICR	495-509
LINO	226-255
LYCE	199-206
MADR	714-719
MOFT	131-152
MORL	423-429
OCLI	555-578
REHV	192-197
SPTR	302-311

Sassoon, Siegfried

HERT	92- 108

Sayers, Dorothy

MUFP	135-142

Scaliger, Julius Caesar

HICR	69- 80

Schehadé, Georges

DIPA	238-243

Schelling, Friedrich

HIMW	74- 82

Scherer, Wilhelm

HIOM	297-303

Schiller, Friedrich

DETR	172-185
HICT	377-384
HIGE	190-200
HIMC	232-255
LAES	3- 95
OBCO	134-186

Schlegel, August

HICT	391-402
HIMW	36- 73

Schlegel, Friedrich

   HICT   391-402

   HIMW   5- 35

Schoenberg, Arnold

   LASI   127-139

Schopenhauer, Arthur

   ESTD   372-410

   HIMW   308-318

Scott, Robert

   BIBM   599-604

Scott, Sir Walter

   AGFI   63- 75

   ARNO   79- 92

   ASPN   51- 62

   CAEN   152-172

   COES   131-143

   DROR   25- 51

   ENNO   113-124

   ENNO   360-369

   HIEL   334-341

   INEN   105-122

   LIES   88-121

LIHE   1207-1218

LIHIC   1207-1218

LINL   51- 67

LODA   160-170

REND   113-130

SELE   209-218

TIPI   96-125

WOVN   57- 68

Seabury, Samuel

   LIHA   334-355

Sedgwick, Anne Douglas

   AMFH   582-595

Sedgwick, Catharine

   RIAN   200-212

Seldes, Gilbert

   SHLI   156-173

Senarens, Luis P.

   EXIN   108-127

Seneca the Elder (Lucius
   Annaeus Seneca)

   HICL   230-240

   LIHRS   37- 53

Seneca the Younger (Lucius
  Annaeus Seneca)

  ANCR   348-353

  CORD   xxxvi-xlvi

  HILL   244-259

  LIHRS   159-222

Servius (Servius Marius
  Honoratus)

  HICL   334-340

Seton, Anya

  CLCO   311-318

Sewall, Samuel

  MACA   88- 97 v.1

Sexton, Anne

  ALWA   442-450

  COAP   218-234

Shakespeare, William

  CHEL   56- 85

  CLCO   161-167

  CLRE   177-186

  COED   287-302

  CRAL   79- 85

  DETR   142-150

ESFI   271-288

HIEL   94-106

IMSC   99-168

LASA   87- 92

LASA   101-124

LASI   198-211

LICR   167-172

LICR   484-494

LIES   1- 25

LIFD   25- 30

LIFD   310-315

LIHE   519-540

LIHIA   519-540

LIWM   34- 41

MADR   212-236

META   40- 72

NOIT   45- 60

POPO   39- 52

POPO   286-292

POPO   302-307

PRTR   86-100

PSLP   219-283

REHP   37-103

REVA   42- 49

Shakespeare, William (cont.)

SELE	74-105
SHEL	313-329
SPTR	165-195
TILI	250-270
WEWU	24- 49
WIHO	164-189
WITS	279-289
WROW	3- 14

Shapiro, Karl

AMPO	53- 68
AMPP	585-596
COAP	101-121

Shaw, George Bernard

AMBL	249-264
BIBM	34- 40
CLCO	238-243
COTH	80-111
ENLT	45- 85
HIEL	460-466
LIFD	127-132
LIHE	1520-1525
LIHIC	1520-1525

LILIC	92-110
MADR	591-616
MOPW	160-196
OCDR	194-206
RIFW	81- 88
TRTH	165-196

Shaw, Irwin

FIFO	106-113

Sheldon, Edward

HIAD	86- 99 v.2

Shelley, Mary Wollstonecraft

EXIN	33- 45

Shelley, Percy Bysshe

COESB	20- 26
CRAL	111-128
HIEL	314-320
LIHE	1230-1240
LIHIC	1230-1240
LISH	417-423
POPO	91- 97
SELE	187-208
TILI	369-378

WIHO	91- 97(b)	CORE	38- 49 v.2
		ENEI	294-319
Sheridan, Richard Brinsley		IDAE	28- 45
POSU	73- 84	IDAE	62- 70
Sherman, William Tecumseh		LIHE	472-480
PAGO	174-210	LIHIA	472-480
		LISH	167-172
Sherwood, Robert			
AMDR	213-225	Silius Italicus	
MOAP	99-117	LIHRS	361-372
Shiel, M. P.		Sillitoe, Alan	
EXIN	142-156	POBF	14- 33
Shoffman, Gershon		Silone, Ignazio	
MATM	111-123	DENE	280-293
		MORL	433-440
Sholokhov, Mikhail Alexandrovich		PISA	109-178
HISL	216-232	PRVM	158-183
INLI	300-305	SHGO	19- 38
RUTH	191-242		
SORL	184-192	Simak, Clifford D.	
VOSN	35- 62(b)	SETO	266-282
Sidney, Sir Philip		Simenon, Georges	
COES	19- 27	NELI	133-150
		WWFS	143-160

Simms, William Gillmore

AMFH	114-123
CAAN	32- 37
MACA	125-136 v.2
RIAN	228-246
WOWI	233-246

Simon, Claude

NEFN	137-145

Simonides

HIGL	184-190
LAGL	99-105

Simpson, Louis

ALWA	451-470

Simpson, Norman Frederick

ANTH	58- 64
THAB	217-224
THPP	212-220

Sinclair, May

LILIC	123-129

Sinclair, Upton

AFGT	37- 47

BOCT	144-151
CACL	317-330(b)
COAM	65- 74
COYE	372-378
RANU	30- 38

Singer, Isaac Bashevis

CONT	283-288
DENE	75- 90
OCLI	579-590
YILI	479-499

Singer, Israel Joshua

YILI	452-478

Singmaster, Elsie

CAAN	299-306

Sitwell, Edith

CEOW	58- 63
LILIC	129-134
POOT	220-228

Sitwell, Sacheverell

LILIC	139-145

Slessor, Kenneth

 ESPO   111-121

Smith, Edward E.

 SETO   9- 26

Smith, Joseph

 BOTC   26- 35

Smith, Logan Pearsall

 BIBM   114-130

Smith, William Jay

 POOP   182-197

Smollett, Tobias George

 BEJA   131-159

 CAEN   69- 77

 LINL   20- 26

 REND   58- 68

Snodgrass, William Dewitt

 ALWA   471-484

 MOAM   351-368

 POPR   92-115

Snow, C. P.

 BEYC   145-177

CONE   62- 84

CONT   171-177

LILIC   153-160

POBF   207-215

Snyder, Gary

 ALWA   485-498

Socrates

 HIGL   493-504

 RHGR   27- 39

 RHGR   162-167

Söderblom, Nathan

 COPT   1- 20

Soffici, Ardengo

 MOIN   176-181

Solger, Karl

 HIMW   298-303

Sologub, Fedor

 RUNO   302-324

Solon

 HIGL   121-128

Solzhenitsyn, Alexander I.

    INLI   321-332

    RUTH   78-118

Sontag, Susan

    CONR   30- 41

    REHV   261-268

Sophocles

    ANCR   182-190

    FRSS   147-163

    GRWA   258-270

    HIGL   271-298

    HIGR   84- 91

    LAGL   136-147

    MADR   40- 55

    PRTR   77- 86

    REHP   111-166

    SPTR   78-102

    TILI   51- 58

    WOBO   272-295

Sorley, Charles Hamilton

    HERT   51- 59

Southey, Robert

    DROR   102-113

Spark, Muriel

    ASPR   304-314

    CONTI   202-216

    OCLI   591-596

Sparks, Jared

    FLNE   124-130

Spencer, Bernard

    MODP   90-100

Spencer, Herbert

    LITR   220-228

Spender, Stephen

    LILIC   167-172

Spenser, Edmund

    ENEI   262-293

    LIHE   483-502

    LIHIA   483-502

    SHEL   264-270

    WIHO   148-159

Spitteler, Carl

    POPO   251-263

Spofford, Harriet Prescott

    AMFH   208-214

Staël, Madame de

    FRLI   41- 49

    HICT   99-109

    HIMW   219-231

Stafford, Jean

    FIFO   294-307

    PICA   152-160

Stafford, William

    ALWA   499-506

Stansbury, Joseph

    LIHAR   80- 96

Stapledon, Olaf

    EXIN   261-277

Starobinski, Jean

    CRCO   165-186

Statius, Publius Papinius

    HILL   271-277

    LIHRS   373-396

Steele, Sir Richard

    LIHE   870-881

    LIHIB   870-881

    SHEL   533-539

Steffens, Lincoln

    BOTC   132-143

    CACL   305-316(b)

Stein, Gertrude

    AXCA   237-256

    CEOW   251-270(b)

    COYE   429-440

    FERE   247-253

    KICA   69- 79

    MONA   83- 89

    RORH   16 0-166(b)

    SHLI   575-586

    WOWE   299-305

Stein, Leo

    COYE   433-443

Steinbeck, John

    AMFI   309-347

    CAAN   443-448

CACL 220-229(b)

CLCO 35- 45

FIMA 369-387

FIYA 217-236

INLI 43- 48

MONA 160-168

NEYT 181-188

NOAM 133-162

NOFI 147-169

NOVA 124-143

WRIC 239-270

Steiner, George
REHV 205-210

Stendhal
ARFI 77-108

CLRE 233-238

CONT 265-271

FRLI 176-184

HIMW 244-252

MAEN 156-166

MIRO 42- 57

POSU 181-200

WITS 149-170

Stephen, Leslie
HIOM 185-190

RIFM 83- 93

Stephens, Alexander H.
MACA 82- 93 v.2
PAGO 380-437

Stephens, James
PLDO 19- 35

Stephens, John L.
WOWI 370-376

Sterne, Laurence
ARNO 69- 78

BEJA 173-192

CAEN 78- 87

CLRE 217-224

COES 95-101

COESA 86- 93

CORE 80- 88 v.2

ENNO 83- 98

ENNO 336-346

INEN 81- 86

LINO 136-159

NOVE	136-159
REND	75- 94

Stevens, Wallace

AMPP	428-442
AWTC	225-232
COCH	190-215
CONTI	77- 91
DAEC	68-102
FIMA	389-423
HIAP	326-335
INDR	431-459
MASM	271-280
MOAM	93-115
MOPE	267-284
MOPE	473-484
MOPO	121-151
MOPR	121-131
ORUN	221-240
ORUN	267-290
PLDO	197-267
POAG	121-134
POMI	183-223
POOT	241-253
PORE	217-284

Stevenson, Robert Louis

CACL	163-173(b)
CAEN	373-385
FAOR	126-171
NOIT	77- 91
SHSE	322-328

Stickney, Trumbull

BIBM	107-113

Stifter, Adalbert

GENO	52- 75

Stiles, Ezra

LIHAR	330-338

Stockton, Francis Richard

AMFH	220-231

Stoddard, Charles W.

TIMW	269-274

Storm, Theodor

ESTD	270-286

Stowe, Harriet Beecher

BOTC	89- 99
CAAN	91-102

Stowe, Harriet Beecher (cont.)

LODA	261-267
MACA	371-378 v. 2
PAGO	3- 65
RIAN	447-463

Strachey, Giles Lytton

BRVL	408-432
ENLT	281-291
LILIC	185-192

Strand, Mark

ALWA	507-516

Strindberg, August

CONR	204-218
COTH	42- 59
GESC	267-274
GESC	583-603
GESC	624-632
MADR	388-396
MOPW	59-106
OCDR	179-192
SPTR	275-280

Sturgeon, Theodore

SETO	229-248

Styron, William

AMMO	239-250
COAN	214-221
CRPR	130-141
LANI	123-137
OCLI	597-606
RAIS	124-133
WWFS	267-282

Suetonius (Gaius Suetonius Tranquillus)

LIHRS	503-512
LITC	vii-xvi

Sullivan, Arthur S.

CLCO	359-365

Supervielle, Jules

COFP	45- 70
MICF	66- 73

Surtees, Robert

CAEN	197-202
LINL	88- 93

Svevo, Italo

    SPLE   171-179

Swados, Harvey

    COAN   183-192

    RAIS   134-140

Swenson, May

    ALWA   517-532

    POOP   147-159

Swift, Jonathan

    BEJA   43- 52

    CLCO   453-459

    COED   205-223

    HIEL   189-194

    LIHE   857-869

    LIHIB   857-869

    SHEL   528-533

Swinburne, Algernon Charles

    BIBM   228-269

    DAPA   19- 35

    HIOM   371-381

    LIHE   1439-1447

    LIHIC   1439-1447

    ROAG   213-267

    WIHO   379-388

Symonds, John Addington

    HIOM   400-407

Symons, Arthur

    DAPA   96-119

Synge, John Millington

    AMBL   328-334

    MADR   553-562

Tacitus, Cornelius

    COWO   ix-xxiii

    HILL   321-330

    LIHRS   447-476

Taggard, Genevieve

    SHLI   345-350

Taine, Hippolyte

    FRLI   265-270

    FRLI   306-313

    HIOM   27- 57

    LICR   406-418

Tanizaki, Junichiró

    FISL   33- 41

Tardieu, Jean

    THAB   168-176

    THPP   84- 97

Tarkington, Booth

    AMFH   596-606

    CAAN   244-251

    COAM   84- 94

    COYE   321-329

    INDA   218-227(b)

    PUPN   32- 39

Tasso, Torquato

    HIIL   268-281

Tate, Allen

    CONTI   91- 99

    HIAP   372-378

    INDR   528-533

    MOMP   93-102

    MOPE   127-138

    POOT   195-202

Taylor, Bayard

RIAN   475-486

TIMW   28- 36

Taylor, Bert Leston

    FAAH   117-124

Taylor, Edward

    AMPP   16- 24

    POMI   54- 81

Taylor, Frederick Winslow

    BOTC   175-184

Taylor, John

    MACA   14- 19 v.2

Taylor, Peter

    AMSS   61- 68

Teasdale, Sara

    HIAP   98-106

Teilhard de Chardin, Pierre

    COPT   77- 84

Tennyson, Alfred Lord

    BRVL   103-130

    HIEL   369-375

Tennyson, Alfred Lord (cont.)

INLA	135-155	
LIHE	1382-1391	
LIHIC	1382-1391	
ORUN	90-107	
SHEL	727-732	
VILI	53- 77	
WEWU	167-177	
WIHO	303-315	

Terence

HILL	44- 50
LIHRO	148-159

Tertz, Abram

RUTH	3- 77

Terzakis, Angelos

FISL	84-103

Thackeray, William
  Makepeace

AGFI	177-203
ARNO	105-116
BRVL	253-266
CAEN	291-297
CLCO	348-358

CLCO	348-358
ENNO	139-152
ENNO	380-390
INEN	156-170
LIHE	1355-1360
LIHIC	1355-1360
MIRO	111-124
NOVE	111-126
POSU	200-216
REND	152-168
VIDE	139-158
VILI	159-181
VINO	60- 99
WOVN	185-197
WOVN	245-260

Theocritus

HIGL	718-726

Thomas Aquinas, Saint

LISH	125-131

Thomas, Augustus

HIAD	239-264 v.1

Thomas, Dylan		Thoreau, Henry David	
CEOW	123-132(b)	AMPP	115-123
CONT	192-200	AMRE	76- 97
INDI	171-186	AMRE	153-175
LIES	50- 61	AMSL	130-139
LILIC	218-224	BOTC	78- 88
MOPE	243-248	COOC	255-264
MOPO	183-191	CYAL	61- 66
MOPR	203-219	EVHO	92-112
OCLI	607-615	FLNE	295-312
PLDO	317-323	FLNE	369-383
POOT	331-344	FRAL	175-231
POPO	151-164	LITR	155-160
PORE	190-216	MACA	400-413 v. 2
PRAB	57- 65	RIFA	363-368
		ROAL	131-139
Thompson, Daniel Pierce		SEPP	295-315
RIAN	270-275	SHRE	208-227
		SHRE	234-243
Thompson, Francis		SHRE	234-243
OPRI	271-290	TEAH	39- 50
		WAFE	108-114
Thompson, Jim		WOEL	84- 90
TOGW	230-238		
Thomson, James		Thucydides	
LIHE	935-942	COWT	ix-xx
LIHIB	935-942	GRWA	184-203

Thucydides (cont.)

HIGL	455-481
HIGR	118-123
LAGL	176-190

Thurber, James

OJBO	29- 40
RIFA	285-290
WWFS	83- 98

Tibullus, Albius

HILL	185-193
LIHRO	403-410

Ticknor, George

FLNE	75- 91

Tieck, Ludwig

HIMW	93-100

Tillich, Paul

COPT	151-157

Tocqueville, Alexis de

BOTC	47- 56

Tolkien, J. R. R.

BIBM	326-332

Tolstoi, Aleksei

HISL	203-215
SORL	40- 50

Tolstoi, Leo Nikolaevich

ARFI	273-299
CLCO	441-452
ESRN	170-214
ESTD	176-188
GRBR	234-308
HIOM	280-291
LASS	38- 54
LASS	134-149
LISH	462-468
LIWM	250-256
MIRO	148-164
OURL	145-157
OPSE	66- 75
REIM	192-216
RUNO	236-273
SPLE	131-145
TILI	411-420
TWDR	45- 56

Tomlinson, Charles
    ORUN   23- 31

Tompkins, J. M. S.
    LINL   176-181

Toomer, Jean
    NENO   80- 89

Tourgée, Albion W.
    PAGO   529-548
    RIAN   521-535

Tozzi, Federico
    MOIN   210-216

Traherne, Thomas
    POPO   53- 60

Trakl, Georg
    COSG   291-323

Traven, B.
    PRWT   114-133

Trilling, Lionel
    FIFO   135-144

Trollope, Anthony
    AGFI   337-343
    CAEN   286-303
    LINL   128-140
    MIRO   165-183
    POSU   217-232
    VIDE   181-193
    VILI   37- 52
    VINO   227-261
    WOVN   322-336

Trotsky, Leon
    LASI   365-380
    REHV   142-147
    SPLE   264-276

Trumbo, Dalton
    PRWT   106-113

Trumbull, John
    LIHA   187-221
    LIHA   427-450

Tucholsky, Kurt
    WHIF   xii-xix

Tucker, Nathaniel Beverley
    MACA   35- 40 v. 2

Tuckerman, Frederick Goddard		AMHU	167-175
COCH	52- 75	AMNF	61- 72
COPF	ix-xxviii	AMNO	137-162
		BEDA	94-115
Tu Fu		CAAN	109-126
CLRE	126-131	CACL	92-102(b)
		CLRE	280-285
Turgenev, Ivan Sergeyevich		CYAL	150-162
ESRN	62- 129	ETAN	51- 67
COES	247-253	EXNO	40- 48
GRBR	64-100	FERE	61- 76
HENR	9- 41	FRWE	82-111
LINL	383-389	HIAD	110-116 v.1
MIRO	127-147	LIOA	708-720
OURL	84- 92	LITR	211-220
REIM	165-173	LODA	384-392
RUNO	119-158	LODA	553-591
		MACA	86-101 v.3
Turner, Frederick Jackson		MASM	180-190
BOTC	122-131	REAP	113-143
VILA	291-304	RIAN	599-652
		RIFA	117-161
Tvardovsky, Alexander		ROAL	223-232
HISL	284-294	SEST	109-117
Twain, Mark			
AMFH	243-256		

SHRE	674-741(b)	EXRE	126-131
TEAH	79-90	FRPC	47- 70
TILI	421-429	GUCF	33- 49
TIMW	291-309	LICA	65- 72
TIMW	459-475	LICR	451-467
TWGA	34- 48	LIOS	322-364
WOEL	175-207	STHT	280-289
		TOCC	35- 42

Tyler, Royall

WITS   201-209

RIAN   60- 68

Vallejo, César Abraham

Unamuno y Jugo,
  Miguel de

POHU   v-xviii(b)

PRTR   56- 62

Van Dine, S. S.

Ungaretti, Giuseppe

MUFP   163-168

GUCI   168-177

Van Doren, Mark

Updike, John

MOMP   75- 83

COAN   207-214

Van Vechten, Carl

CONR   62- 68

NEVA   157-163

Valerius Maximus

Van Vogt, A. E.

LIHRS   54- 66

SETO   213-228

Valéry, Paul

Vargas Llosa, Mario

AXCA   64- 92

COFP   13- 43

INMA   342-376

Varro, Marcus Terentius

    LIHRO   241-252

Vauquelin de la Fresnaye, Jean

    HICR   128-134

Veblen, Thorstein

    FERE   156-162

Vega, Lope de

    MADR   177-185

    MERS   57- 73

Velleius Paterculus, Gaius

    LIHRS   68- 81

Verga, Giovanni

    HIIL   452-457

    LINL   320-327

    MOIN   23- 29

Verlaine, Paul

    TILI   352-362(b)

Verne, Jules

    EXIN   73- 87

Very, Jones

AMPP   123-129

INDR   262-282

Vestdijk, Simon

    FISL   145-152

Vico, Giambattista

    HIIL   334-341

Vida, Marco Girolamo

    HICR   29- 37

Vigny, Alfred de

    FRLI   122-128

    LINL   376-382

    STHT   224-247

Villa, Jose Garcia

    NEWP   103-111

Villon, François

    CLGR   80- 88

    COWF   ix-xv

    COWF   xvii-xxiii(b)

    TEFV   ix-xxxvi(b)

    TEFV   117-157(b)

    TEFV   157-180

TILI	185-208	Vonnegut, Kurt		
		FABU	46- 55	
Virgil				
ANCR	337-342	Voznesensky, Andrei		
ENEI	67- 87	ANFC	xiii-xxiii	
HICL	324-340	ANTI	ix-xviii	
HILL	140-163			
LACL	206-287	Wagner, Richard		
		SPTR	252-259	
LERBL	443-450			
LIHRO	318-362	Wagoner, David		
OPPO	135-148	ALWA	533-551	
POPO	245-250			
		Wain, John		
TILI	107-119	POBF	128-144	
WIHO	65- 74			
		Walker, Francis A.		
Vittorini, Elio		MACA	111-117 v.3	
GUCI	87-113			
		Wallant, Edward Lewis		
Voltaire (François-Marie Arouet)		LANI	138-151	
CAOW	ix-xx	MIAN	118-137	
HIMC	31- 45			
POSU	98-108	Walpole, Horace		
POVO	1- 37(b)	COESA	105-117	
POVO	37- 51	POSU	84- 98	
PRTR	130-136			

Walpole, Hugh		TWGA 177-198
LILIC	281-287	WWFS 183-207
Ward, Douglas Turner		Wasson, R. Gordon
BLAWP	150-155	BIBM 339-354
Ward, Elizabeth Stuart Phelps		Waugh, Alec
AMFH	192-203	NEYT 314-319
Ward, Nathaniel		Waugh, Evelyn
MACA	76- 81 v.1	CLCO 140-146
		CLCO 298-305
Warren, Robert Penn		CONE 167-182
AMPP	543-559	LILIC 301-309
ETAN	177-186	SHGO 67- 89
FIFO	198-229	VAHE 23- 44
FIYA	274-284	WWTS 103-114
LANI	16- 34	
LUGD	81-110	Webber, Charles W.
MOMP	114-119	VILA 78- 84
MOPE	111-120	
NEYT	307-313	Webster, Daniel
NOIT	119-133	MACA 304-316 v.2
NOVA	86-105	Webster, John
OCLI	616-633	CLRE 186-191
PUPN	132-137	MADR 258-263

Wiedlé, Wladimir

   NELI   151-160

Weinbaum, Stanley G.

   EXIN   296-312

Weisinger, Mortimer

   SETO   102-117

Weiss, Peter

   AGIN   163-174

   MOWO   63- 70

Weiss, Theodore

   ALWA   552-574

   POOP   212-224

Wellek, René

   LASA   493-499

Wells, Herbert George

   AMBL   206-212

   CAEN   458-476

   ENLT   139-160

   EXIN   128-141

   INENO   89- 95

   LILIC   319-326

   LINL   161-169

Welty, Eudora

   CEOW   284-290(b)

   COAN   41- 48

   CRPR   173-192

   FIFO   258-283

   SEES   156-169

Wesker, Arnold

   ANTH   143-158

   MOBD   71- 82

   THPP   234-243

West, Nathanael

   CACL   344-356(b)

   LINL   276-282

   LODA   461-467

   MIAN   81- 94

   SEMA   226-263

   TRWO   213-218

Wharton, Edith

   AMFH   550-581

   AMNF   117-132

   AMNO   273-280

Wharton, Edith (cont.)

ARNO	196-205
AWTC	19- 24
CAAN	252-266
CLCO	413-418
COAM	95-104
COYE	275-293
DENE	122-136
FERE	141-147
FIYA	15- 32
LINL	269-275
MASM	145-153
MONA	12- 22
PICA	20- 55
POSU	247-270
SEMA	11- 45
TRWO	129-147
TWGA	68- 86
WOBO	195-213
WOEL	215-235

Wheelright, John Brooks

HIAP	347-353

Whipple, T. K.

CLCO	70- 80

Whitehead, Alfred North

COPT	51- 62

Whitman, Walt

AMHU	137-145
AMPP	150-180
AMRE	517-625
AMSL	196-205
BEDA	79- 93
COCH	23- 51
CYAL	99-110
EVHO	44- 62
FRAL	397-441
HACR	25- 49
HENR	3- 8
HIOM	191-200
INDI	187-204
INDR	577-603
LICR	195-210
LIES	62- 87
LINL	225-232
LIOA	598-621
LITR	186-196

MACA	69- 86 v.3	Whittemore, Reed	
MAPO	33- 40	POOP	198-211
MAWH	35- 75	Whittier, John Greenleaf	
MOAM	1- 17	AMPP	69- 83
NEYT	70- 76	AMSL	157-164
NOIT	61- 75	COOC	276-283
OTIN	66- 72	COPO	xi-xix(b)
POAG	101-120	FLNE	407-414
POMI	82- 90	LIOA	347-355
POPO	106 -113	MACA	361-370 v.2
REAP	113-143	Wiesel, Elie	
RIFA	385-390	AFTR	151-160
ROAL	159-169		
SHRE	1061-1077	Wilbur, Richard	
STCA	163-177	AMPO	93-106
TEAH	51- 66	AMPP	596-604
TIMW	125-144	COAP	160-175
TIMW	180-196	POOP	160-171
TIMW	223-240	POPR	59- 72
TIMW	452-458	Wilde, Oscar	
TRWO	3- 35	BRVL	481-490
WAFE	203-209	CLCO	331-342
WAFE	239-244	DAPA	53- 80
WIHO	348-362	HIOM	407-416

147

Wilde, Oscar (cont.)

    MOWO   71- 77

Wilder, Thornton

    AMPL   66- 75

    CLCO   81- 86

    IMTR   248-308

    MOAP   204-224

    SHLI   384-391

    SHLI   587-592

    WWFS   99-118

Wilkins, Mary E. see
    Freeman, Mary Wilkins

Williams, Charles

    LILIC   342-348

Williams, Jesse Lynch

    HIAD   68- 74 v. 2

Williams, Roger

    MACA   62- 75 v.1

Williams, Tennessee

    AMDS   18- 39

    AMPL   53- 65

    AMSS   102-111

    COTH   286-293

    MOAP   225-246

    MOPW   335-377

    OCLI   55- 60

Williams, William Carlos

    AMPP   369-386

    EVHO   228-245

    HIAP   207-216

    INDI   171-186

    LASA   282-291

    MOAM   116-153

    MOMP   1- 17

    MOPE   340-358

    MOPR   113-121

    ORUN   180-193

    PLDO   286-296

    POAG   215-226

    POMI   125-161

    POOT   99-111

    PORE   285-359

    WWTS   5- 30

Williamson, Jack

    SETO   84-100

Willis, N. P.

    DEAS   78- 88

    WOWI   338-346

Wilson, Angus

    CONE   244-249

    LILIC   357-363

    POBF   145-164

    WWFS   251-266

Wilson, Edmund

    CONTI   100-116

Wilson, Harry L.

    CACL   331-343(b)

Windsor, Edward

    KICA   35- 41

Winters, Yvor

    LISH   669-676

    MODP   64- 74

Winthrop, John

    MACA   38- 50 v.1

Winthrop, Theodore

    RIAN   487-494

    TIMW   118-124

Wirt, William

    MACA   30- 35 v.2

Witherspoon, John

    LIHAR   319-330

Wittgenstein, Ludwig J. J.

    MOWO   130-135

Wittig, Monique

    WROW   102-111

Wodehouse, P. G.

    COEC   341-355

    LILIC   366-371

Wolfe, Thomas

    AFGT   159-166

    AMDA   149-157

    AMFI   173-215

    AMMO   119-144

    AMNF   206-218

    AMNO   343-348

    CAAN   409-415

    CYAL   263-269

Wolfe, Thomas (cont.)

EVHO	9- 18	LISY	158-163
FIMA	425-456	MOBF	376-433
FIYA	197-215	MOWO	38- 46
MONA	180-187	NOMW	187-217
NOAM	110-132	NOVE	262-279
NOVA	52- 68	VAHE	170-186
SEES	170-183	WITS	65- 88
SEMA	189-225		
TEAH	147-155		

Woollcott, Alexander

CLCO 87- 93

THBU 342-347

Woolman, John

WRIC 187-235

LIHAR 340-347

LIOA 124-129

Wolfert, Ira

PRWT 177-182

Woolson, Constance Fenimore

AMFH 332-342

Wollstonecraft, Mary see
Godwin, Mary Wollstone-
craft

RIAN 568-578

TIMW 351-360

Woolf, Virginia

Wordsworth, William

ARNO	328-337	HICT	200-218
CAEN	522-532	HIEL	291-301
ENLT	245-253	HIMW	130-150
IMSC	378-392	LICR	141-160
INENO	100-110	LIHE	1136-1148
LILIC	379-387		

LIHIC	1136-1148	DENE	169-177
LISH	345-352	NASO	65- 86
LISH	401-409	NENO	140-152
MASM	86-100	NEVA	222-234
OBCO	34- 79	NOAM	226-253
OPSE	118-150	REHV	122-132
POPO	228-235	SHAC	77- 94
WEWU	124-150		
WIHO	233-251	Wycherley, William	
		FIMC	38- 44
Wouk, Herman		FIMC	64- 85
AMMO	38- 45	FIMC	96-113
MAMF	134-146	REDR	105-138
PUPN	158-164		
		Wylie, Elinor	
Wright, Austin Tappan		HIAP	282-291
BPSW	233-243(b)	MOMP	35- 40
Wright, James		Wylie, Philip	
ALWA	575-586	EXIN	278-295
COAP	197-217		
		Wyndham, John	
Wright, Judith		SETO	118-132
ESPO	158-176		
		Xenophon	
Wright, Richard		ENEI	51- 59
BLAW	125-141	GRWA	204-226

Xenophon (cont.)

   HIGL   616-623

   HIGR   123-129

Yates, Richard

   REHV   44- 49

Yeats, William Butler

   AMBL   311-317

   AXCA   26- 63

   COEB   271-276

   INDI   87-114

   KICA   42- 48

   LILIC   388-397

   LISH   597-606

   LISY   247-253

   MOPE   54- 67

   MOPE   395-446

   MOPE   501-520

   MOPO   15- 28

   MOPR   28- 48

   OPPO   295-308

   ORUN   108-145

   POEX   115-147

   POOT   254-278

POPO   122-128

PORE   68-130

PRAB   30- 39

WEWU   178-191

Yehoash

   YILI   165-181

Yesenin, Sergey

   HISL   69- 83

Yevtushenko, Yevgeny

   HISL   328-339

   INLI   334-340

   POYY   x-xxxvii

   SELP   8- 18

   YESP   8- 17

Yizhar, S.

   AFTR   210-225

Zamyatin, Evgeny

   HISL   84- 96

   RUTH   288-297

   SORL   80- 89

Zeitlin, Hillel

    MATM   100-111

Zeno (Stoic Philosopher)

    ANCR   245-252

    ECGR   157-164

    FONN   89- 94

Zevi, Sabbatai

    AFTR   63- 75

Zola, Emile

    HENR   139-168

    HIOM   14- 22

Zoshchenko, Mikhail

    HISL   97-109

    SORL   90- 96

Zuccoli, Luciano

    MOIN   87- 93

KEY TO SYMBOLS WITH BOOKS ANALYZED

AFGT
Cowley, Malcolm, ed.
After the genteel tradition.
Carbondale, Southern Ill. Univ. Press, 1964.

AFTE
McCormack, Thomas, comp.
Afterwords.
New York, Harper, 1968.

AFTR
Alter, Robert
After the tradition.
New York, Dutton, 1969.

AGFI
Karl, Frederick R.
An age of fiction.
New York, Farrar, Straus, 1964.

AGIN
Sontag, Susan
Against interpretation and other essays.
New York, Farrar, Straus, 1966.

ALWA
Howard, Richard
Alone with America.
New York, Atheneum Pubs., 1969.

AMBL
Van Doren, Carl and Mark Van Doren
American and British literature since 1890.
New York, Appleton, 1967.

AMDA
Madden, David, ed.
American dreams, American nightmares.
Carbondale, Southern Ill. Univ. Press, 1970.

AMDR
Krutch, Joseph Wood
American drama since 1918.
New York, Braziller, 1957.

AMDS
Weales, Gerald
American drama since World War II.
New York, Harcourt, 1962.

AMEI	Ziff, Larzer The American 1890's. New York, Viking, 1966.
AMFH	Quinn, Arthur Hobson American fiction: an historical and critical survey. New York, Appleton, 1964.
AMFI	Beach, Joseph Warren American fiction, 1920-1940. New York, Russell & Russell, 1960.
AMHU	Rourke, Constance American humor. Garden City, N. Y., Doubleday, 1931.
AMLA	The American literary anthology, v. 1. New York, Farrar, Straus, 1968.
AMLI	The American literary anthology, v. 2. New York, Random, 1969.
AMMO	Geismar, Maxwell American moderns. New York, Hill & Wang, 1958.
AMNF	Stegner, Wallace, ed. The American novel: from James Fenimore Cooper to William Faulkner. New York, Basic Bks., 1965.
AMNO	Van Doren, Carl The American novel, 1789-1939. New York, Macmillan, 1940.
AMPL	Lewis, Allan American plays and playwrights of the con- temporary theatre. New York, Crown, 1965.
AMPO	Stepanchev, Stephen American poetry since 1945. New York, Harper, 1965.
AMPP	Waggoner, Hyatt H. American poets from the Puritans to the present. Boston, Houghton, 1968.

AMRE   Matthiessen, F. O.
American renaissance.
New York, Oxford, 1941.

AMSL   Perry, Bliss
American spirit in literature.
London, Oxford, 1921.

AMSS   Peden, William
The American short story.
Cambridge, Houghton, 1964.

ANCR   Hadas, Moses
Ancilla to classical reading.
Morningside Heights, N. Y., Columbia Univ.
     Press, 1954.

ANFC   Voznesensky, Andrei
Antiworlds and the fifth ace.
New York, Anchor Bks., 1967.

ANGH   Fowlie, Wallace
Andre Gide: his life and art.
New York, Macmillan, 1965.

ANTH   Taylor, John Russell
The angry theatre.
New York, Hill & Wang, 1962.

ANTI   Voznesensky, Andrei
Antiworlds
New York, Basic Bks., 1966.

APTC   Unterecker, John, ed.
Approaches to the twentieth-century novel.
New York, Crowell, 1965.

ARDO   Cohen, Arthur A.
Arguments and doctrines.
New York, Harper, 1970.

ARFI   Maugham, W. Somerset
The art of fiction.
Garden City, N. Y., Doubleday, 1955.

ARIS   Aristotle
Aristotle: selections.
New York, Scribner, 1938.

ARNO   Edgar, Pelham
The art of the novel: from 1700 to the present time.
New York, Russell & Russell, 1965.

ASPN   Forster, E. M.
Aspects of the novel.
New York, Harcourt, 1927.

ASPR   Updike, John
Assorted prose.
New York, Knopf, 1965.

AWTC   Thorp, William W.
American writing in the twentieth century.
Cambridge, Mass., Harvard Univ. Press, 1960.

AXCA   Wilson, Edmund
Axel's castle.
New York, Scribner, 1931.

BABY   Dickey, James
Babel to Byzantium; poets and poetry now.
New York, Farrar, Straus, 1968.

BASP   Casona, Alejandro
La banca sin pescador.
New York, Oxford, 1955.

BAVE   Peguy, Charles
Basic verities; prose and poetry.
New York, Pantheon Bks., 1943.

BAWA   Aristotle
The basic works of Aristotle.
New York, Random House, 1941.

BAWC   Cicero, Marcus Tullius
The basic works of Cicero.
New York, Modern Library, 1951.

BEDA   Jones, Howard Mumford
Belief and disbelief in American literature.
Chicago, Univ. of Chicago Press, 1967.

BEJA   Steeves, Harrison R.
Before Jane Austen...
New York, Holt, 1965.

BEPR   Racine, Jean
       The best plays of Racine.
       Princeton, Princeton Univ. Press, 1957.

BEYC   Trilling, Lionel
       Beyond culture.
       New York, Viking, 1965.

BIBM   Wilson, Edmund
       The bit between my teeth.
       New York, Farrar, Straus, 1965.

BINA   Buckman, Thomas R., ed.
       Bibliography & natural history.
       Lawrence, Univ. of Kansas Libraries, 1966.

BLAW   Bigsby, C. W. E., ed.
       The black American writer, v. 1: Fiction.
       Deland, Fla., Everett/Edwards, Inc., 1969.

BLAWP   Bigsby, C. W. E., ed.
       The black American writer, v. 2: Poetry and
         drama.
       Deland, Fla., Everett/Edwards, Inc., 1969.

BLES   Brieux, Eugene
       Blanchette and the escape...
       Boston, John W. Luce & Co., 1913.

BOGL   Ruiz, Juan
       The book of good love.
       Chapel Hill, Univ. of N. C. Press, 1968.

BOML   Miller, Henry
       The books in my life.
       New York, New Directions, 1952.

BOTC   Downs, Robert B.
       Books that changed America.
       New York, Macmillan, 1970.

BPSW   Powell, Lawrence Clark
       Bookman's progress.
       Los Angeles, Ward Ritchie Press, 1968.

BREA   Malin, Irving and Irwin Stark
       Breakthrough.
       New York, McGraw, 1964.

BRVL   Kumar, Shiv K., ed.
British Victorian literature.
New York, N. Y. Univ. Press, 1969.

CAAN   Wagenknecht, Edward
Cavalcade of the American novel.
New York, Holt, 1952.

CACL   Powell, Lawrence Clark
California classics: the creative literature of
   the golden state.
Los Angeles, Ward Ritchie Press, 1971.

CAEN   Wagenknecht, Edward
Cavalcade of the English novel.
New York, Holt, 1954.

CANT   Guillen, Jorge
Cantico.
Boston, Little, 1965.

CAOW   Voltaire, François Marie Arouet de
Candide and other writings.
New York, Modern Library, 1956.

CEOW   Porter, Katherine Anne
Collected essays and occasional writings...
New York, Delacorte Press, 1970.

CHEL   Gillie, Christopher
Character in English literature.
New York, Barnes & Noble, 1965.

CHPC   Corneille, Pierre
The chief plays of Corneille.
Princeton, Princeton Univ. Press, 1957.

CLCO   Wilson, Edmund
Classics and commercials.
New York, Farrar, Straus, 1950.

CLGR   Fowlie, Wallace
The clown's grail.
Denver, Alan Swallow, 1948.

CLRE   Rexroth, Kenneth
Classics revisited.
Chicago, Quadrangle Bks., 1968.

COAM	Van Doren, Carl Contemporary American novelists, 1900-1920. New York, Macmillan, 1922.
COAN	Moore, Harry T., ed. Contemporary American novelists. Carbondale, Southern Ill. Univ. Press, 1964.
COAP	Mills, Ralph, Jr. Contemporary American poetry. New York, Random House, 1965.
COCH	Donoghue, Denis Connoisseurs of chaos. New York, 1965.
COEA	Orwell, George Collected essays..., vol. 1: An age like this, 1920-1940. New York, Harcourt, 1968.
COEB	Orwell, George Collected essays..., vol. 2: My country right or left, 1940-1943. New York, Harcourt, 1968.
COEC	Orwell, George Collected essays..., vol. 3: As I please, 1943-1945. New York, Harcourt, 1968.
COED	Orwell, George Collected essays..., vol. 4: In front of your nose, 1945-1950. New York, Harcourt, 1968.
COEN	Mandel, Siegfried, ed. Contemporary European novelists. Carbondale, Southern Ill. Univ. Press, 1968.
COES	Woolf, Virginia Collected essays, v. 1. New York, Harcourt, 1966.
COESA	Woolf, Virginia Collected essays, v. 3. New York, Harcourt, 1967.

COESB	Woolf, Virginia Collected essays, v. 4. New York, Harcourt, 1967.
COFP	Chiari, Joseph Contemporary French poetry. Freeport, N. Y., Books for Libraries Press, 1952.
COMF	Adereth, M. Commitment in modern French literature. New York, Schocken Bks., 1967.
CONE	Karl, Frederick R. The contemporary English novel. New York, Noonday Press, 1962.
CONR	Gilman, Richard The confusion of realms. New York, Random House, 1969.
CONT	Kazin, Alfred Contemporaries. Boston, Little, 1962.
CONTI	Kermode, Frank Continuities. New York, Random House, 1968.
COOC	Vogel, Stanley M., ed. An outline of American literature, v. 1: Colonial origins to the Civil War. Boston, Student Outlines Co., 1961.
COPF	Tuckerman, Frederick Goddard Complete poems of Frederick Goddard Tuckerman. New York, Oxford, 1965.
COPO	Whittier, John Greenleaf Complete poetical works... Boston, Houghton, 1894.
COPS	Buonarroti, Michel Angelo Complete poems and selected letters of Michelangelo. New York, Modern Library, 1963.

COPT   Curtis, C. J.
Contemporary Protestant thought.
New York, Bruce Pub., 1970.

COPW   Lowell, James Russell
Complete poetical works of James Russell
    Lowell.
Boston, Houghton, 1925.

CORD   Duckworth, George E., ed.
The complete Roman drama, v. 1.
New York, Random House, 1942.

CORE   Woolf, Virginia
The common reader. First and second series
    combined in one volume.
New York, Harcourt, 1948.

COSG   Hamburger, Michael
Contraries; studies in German literature.
New York, Dutton, 1970.

COTH   Lewis, Allan
The contemporary theatre.
New York, Crown, 1962.

COWF   Villon, François
The complete works of François Villon.
New York, McKay, 1960.

COWO   Tacitus, Cornelius
The complete works of Tacitus.
New York, Modern Library, 1942.

COWT   Thucydides
The complete writings of Thucydides; the
    Peloponnesian War.
New York, Modern Library, 1934.

COYE   Brooks, Van Wyck
The confident years: 1885-1915.
New York, Dutton, 1955.

CRAL   Daiches, David
Critical approaches to literature.
Englewood Cliffs, N. J., Prentice-Hall,
    1956.

CRCO   Lawall, Sarah N.
Critics of consciousness.
Cambridge, Harvard Univ. Press, 1968.

CRID   Garland, Hamlin
Crumbling idols.
Cambridge, Harvard Univ. Press, 1960.

CRPR   Balakian, Nona and Charles Simmons, eds.
The creative present.
New York, Doubleday, 1963.

CYAL   Spiller, Robert E.
The cycle of American literature.
New York, Macmillan, 1956.

DAEC   Blackmur, R. P.
The double agent; essays in craft and
elucidation.
Magnolia, Mass., Peter Smith, 1962.

DAPA   Charlesworth, Barbara
Dark passages; the decadent consciousness in
Victorian literature.
Madison, Univ. of Wis. Press, 1965.

DEAS   Pattee, Fred Lewis
The development of the American short
story.
New York, Biblo & Tannen, 1966.

DENE   Howe, Irving
Decline of the new.
New York, Harcourt, 1970.

DETR   Steiner, George
The death of tragedy.
New York, Knopf, 1961.

DICO   Dante Alighieri
The divine comedy.
New York, Holt, 1954.

DIEP   Epictetus
The discourses of Epictetus; with the
Encheiridion and fragments.
New York, Crowell.

164

DIMN Ziolkowski, Theodore
Dimensions of the modern novel; German texts
 and European contexts.
Princeton, Princeton Univ. Press, 1969.

DIPA Fowlie, Wallace
Dionysus in Paris.
New York, Meridian Bks., 1960.

DIVC Dante Alighieri
The divine comedy, v. 3 & 4.
(Works of Henry Wadsworth Longfellow, v. 9
 & 10).
New York, National Library Co., 1909.

DOPE Perez Galdos, Benito
Dona Perfecta.
New York, Dell Pubs., 1965.

DOPY Miller, Liam
The Dolmen Press Yeats centenary papers
 MCMLXV.
Dublin, The Dolmen Press, 1968.

DREA Borges, Jorge Luis
Dreamtigers.
Austin, Univ. of Tex. Press, 1964.

DROR Chandler, Alice
A dream of order.
Lincoln, Univ. of Neb. Press, 1970.

ECGR Hamilton, Edith
The echo of Greece.
New York, Norton, 1957.

EISP Starkie, Walter, tr.
Eight Spanish plays of the golden age.
New York, Modern Library, 1964.

ELCO Aristophanes
The eleven comedies.
New York, Horace Liveright, 1928.

ELFI Scholes, Robert
Elements of fiction.
New York, Oxford, 1968.

ENEI   Tillyard, E. M.
The English epic and its background.
New York, Barnes & Noble, 1954.

ENLT   Cunliffe, J. W.
English literature in the twentieth century.
Freeport, N. Y., Books for Libraries Press,
1967.

ENNO   Van Ghent, Dorothy
The English novel: form and function.
New York, Holt, 1953.

EPLA   Torres-Rioseco, Arturo
The epic of Latin American literature.
Berkeley, Univ. of Calif. Press, 1942.

ERGO   The era of Goethe; essays presented to James
Boyd.
Freeport, N. Y., Books for Libraries Press,
1968.

ESFD   Tate, Allen
Essays of four decades.
Chicago, Swallow Press, 1968.

ESFI   Priestley, J. B.
Essays of five decades.
Boston, Little, 1968.

ESPO   Buckley, Vincent
Essays in poetry, mainly Australian.
Freeport, N. Y., Books for Libraries Press,
1969.

ESRN   Phelps, William Lyon
Essays on Russian novelists.
New York, Macmillan, 1911.

ESTD   Mann, Thomas
Essays of three decades.
New York, Knopf, 1947.

ETAN   Noble, David W.
The eternal Adam and the new world garden;
the central myth in the American novel
since 1830.
New York, Braziller, 1968.

EUON   Pushkin, Alexander
        Eugene Onegin, v. 3.
        New York, Bollingen Series LXXII, Pantheon
            Bks., 1964.

EVHO   Van Nostrand, A. D.
        Everyman his own poet; romantic gospels in
            American literature.
        New York, McGraw, 1968.

EVPP   Hamilton, Edith
        The ever present past.
        New York, Norton, 1964.

EVRR   Evergreen Review
        Evergreen Review reader, 1957-1967; a ten-
            year anthology.
        New York, Grove, 1968.

EXIN   Moskowitz, Sam
        Explorers of the infinite; shapers of science
            fiction.
        Cleveland, World Pub., 1963.

EXNO   English Institute
        Experience in the novel.
        New York, Columbia Univ. Press, 1968.

EXRE   Cowley, Malcolm
        Exile's return; a literary odyssey of the
            1920's.
        New York, Viking, 1963.

FAAH   Allen, Everett S.
        Famous American humorous poets.
        New York, Dodd, 1968.

FABU   Scholes, Robert
        The fabulators.
        New York, Oxford, 1967.

FAOR   Wallace, Irving
        The fabulous originals; lives of extraordinary
            people who inspired memorable characters
            in fiction.
        New York, Knopf, 1955.

FERE Berthoff, Warner
The ferment of realism; American literature,
 1884-1919.
New York, Free Press, 1965.

FIBG Rabelais, Francois
The five books of Gargantua and Pantagruel
 in the modern translation of Jacques LeClerq.
New York, Modern Library, 1936.

FIFO Eisinger, Chester E.
Fiction of the forties.
Chicago, Univ. of Chicago Press, 1963.

FIMA Bryer, Jackson R.
Fifteen modern American authors.
Durham, Duke Univ. Press, 1969.

FIMC Holland, Norman N.
The first modern comedies; the significance
 of Etherege, Wycherley and Congreve.
Cambridge, Harvard Univ. Press, 1959.

FIPL Munk, Kaj
Five plays.
New York, American-Scandinavian Foundation,
 1953.

FISL Peyre, Henri, ed.
Fiction in several languages.
Boston, Houghton, 1968.

FIYA Gardiner, Harold C.
Fifty years of the American novel; a
 Christian appraisal.
New York, Gordian Press, 1951.

FLJB Kenner, Hugh
Flaubert, Joyce and Beckett; the stoic
 comedians.
Boston, Beacon Press, 1962.

FLNE Brooks, Van Wyck
The flowering of New England.
New York, Dutton, 1952.

FONN   Robbe-Grillet, Alain
For a new novel; essays on fiction.
New York, Grove, 1965.

FOPP   Grossvogel, David L.
Four playwrights and a postscript.
Ithaca, N. Y., Cornell Univ. Press, 1962.

FRAL   Fussell, Edwin
Frontier: American literature and the American West.
Princeton, Princeton Univ. Press, 1965.

FRLH   O'Brien, Justin
The French literary horizon.
New Brunswick, N. J., Rutgers Univ. Press, 1967.

FRLI   Thibaudet, Albert
French literature from 1795 to our era.
New York, Funk, 1967.

FRPC   Maurois, Andre
From Proust to Camus.
Garden City, N. Y., Doubleday, 1966.

FRSB   Bertocci, Angelo Philip
From symbolism to Baudelaire.
Carbondale, Southern Ill. Univ. Press, 1964.

FRSS   Hamburger, Kate
From Sophocles to Sartre; figures from Greek tragedy, classical and modern.
New York, Ungar, 1969.

FRWE   Lee, Robert Edson
From West to East.
Urbana, Univ. of Ill. Press, 1966.

FSFH   Goldhurst, William
F. Scott Fitzgerald and his contemporaries.
Cleveland, World Pub., 1963.

GAWA   Caesar, Julius
The Gallic War and other writings.
New York, Modern Library, 1957.

GEDN Villas, James
 Gerard de Nerval; a critical bibliography,
  1900-1967.
 Columbia, Univ. of Mo. Press, 1968.

GEML Natan, Alex, ed.
 Essays on contemporary German literature,
  v. 4: German men of letters.
 Chester Springs, Pa., Dufour, 1966.

GENO Pascal, Roy
 The German novel.
 Toronto, Univ. of Toronto Press, 1956.

GESC Sprinchorn, Evert, ed.
 The genius of the Scandinavian theater.
 New York, New Am. Lib., 1964.

GOFA Goethe, Johann Wolfgang von
 Goethe's Faust.
 Garden City, N. Y., Doubleday, 1961.

GRBR Davis, Ruth
 The great books of Russia.
 Norman, Univ. of Okla Press, 1968.

GRCR Smith, James Harry and Edd Winfield Parks,
  eds.
 The great critics.
 New York, Norton, 1951.

GRTR Leavis, F. R.
 The great tradition: George Eliot, Henry
  James, Joseph Conrad.
 New York, N. Y. Univ. Press, 1964.

GRWA Hamilton, Edith
 The Greek way.
 New York, Norton, 1942.

GUCF Fowlie, Wallace
 A guide to contemporary French literature:
  from Valery to Sartre.
 Cleveland, World Pub., 1957.

GUCI   Pacifici, Sergio
A guide to contemporary Italian literature;
    from futurism to neorealism.
Cleveland, World Pub., 1962.

GYBA   Garcia Lorca, Federico
The Gypsy ballads of Federico Garcia Lorca.
Bloomington, Ind. Univ. Press, 1953.

HACR   Van Doren, Mark
The happy critic and other essays.
New York, Hill & Wang, 1961.

HEMP   Neruda, Pablo
The heights of Macchu Picchu.
New York, Farrar, Strauss, 1966.

HENR   Richardson, Lyon N.
Henry James; representative selections, with
    introduction, bibliography, and notes.
New York, American Book Co., 1941.

HERT   Bergonzi, Bernard
Heroes' twilight; a study of the literature of
    the Great War.
New York, Coward-McCann, 1965.

HIAD   Quinn, Arthur Hobson
A history of the American drama from the
    Civil War to the present day. (2 vols. in
    one, individual pagination)
New York, Appleton, 1936.

HIAM   Quinn, Arthur Hobson
A history of the American drama from the
    beginning to the Civil War.
New York, Appleton, 1943.

HIAP   Gregory, Horace and Marya Zaturenska
A history of American poetry, 1900-1940.
New York, Gordian Press, 1969.

HICL   Saintsbury, George
A history of criticism and literary taste in
    Europe, v. 1: Classical and mediaeval
    criticism.
Edinburgh, William Blackwood & Sons, Ltd.,
    1961.

HICR   Saintsbury, George
A history of criticism and literary taste in
     Europe, v. 2: from the Renaissance to the
     decline of Eighteenth Century orthodoxy.
Edinburgh, William Blackwood & Sons, Ltd.,
     1967.

HICT   Saintsbury, George
A history of criticism and literary taste in
     Europe, v. 3: modern criticism.
Edinburgh, William Blackwood & Sons, Ltd.,
     1961.

HIEL   Albert, Edward
A history of English literature.
London, George G. Harrap & Co., Ltd., 1955.

HIGE   Rose, Ernst
A history of German literature.
New York, N. Y. Univ. Press, 1960.

HIGL   Lesky, Albin
A history of Greek literature.
New York, Crowell, 1963.

HIGR   Hadas, Moses
A history of Greek literature.
New York, Columbia Univ. Press, 1950.

HIIL   Wilkins, Ernest Hatch
A history of Italian literature.
Cambridge, Harvard Univ. Press, 1954.

HILL   Hadas, Moses
A history of Latin literature.
New York, Columbia Univ. Press, 1952.

HIMC   Wellek, Rene
A history of modern criticism: 1750-1950, v.
     1: the later Eighteenth Century.
New Haven, Yale Univ. Press, 1955.

HIMW   Wellek, Rene
A history of modern criticism: 1750-1950,
     v. 2: the romantic age.
New Haven, Yale Univ. Press, 1955.

HIOC   Wellek, Rene
A history of modern criticism: 1750-1950,
    v. 3: the age of transition.
New Haven, Yale Univ. Press, 1965.

HIOM   Wellek, Rene
A history of modern criticism: 1750-1950,
    v. 4: the later Nineteenth Century.
New Haven, Yale Univ. Press, 1965.

HISL   Alexandrova, Vera
A history of Soviet literature.
Garden City, N. Y., Doubleday, 1963.

HIWL   Cohen, J. M.
A history of western literature.
Chicago, Aldine Publishing Co., 1963.

IDAE   Davis, Walter R.
Idea and act in Elizabethan fiction.
Princeton, Princeton Univ. Press, 1969.

ILLU   Benjamin, Walter
Illuminations.
New York, Harcourt, 1955.

IMSC   Bentley, Eric, ed.
Importance of Scrutiny.
New York, N. Y. Univ. Press, 1948.

IMTR   Wescott, Glenway
Images of truth; remembrances and criticism.
New York, Harper, 1962.

INAR   Aristotle
Introduction to Aristotle.
New York, Modern Library, 1947.

INDA   Wilson, William E.
Indiana: a history.
Bloomington, Indiana Univ. Press, 1966.

INDI   Shapiro, Karl
In defense of ignorance.
New York, Random House, 1960.

INDR   Winters, Yvor
In defense of reason.
Denver, Alan Swallow, 1947.

173

INEN   Kettle, Arnold
       An introduction to the English novel, v. 1:
         Defoe to George Eliot.
       New York, Harper, 1960.

INENO   Kettle, Arnold
       An introduction to the English novel, v. 2:
         Henry James to the present.
       New York, Harper, 1960.

INLA   McLuhan, Marshall
       The interior landscape.
       New York, McGraw, 1969.

INLI   Durant, Will and Ariel Durant
       Interpretations of life.
       New York, Simon & Schuster, 1970.

INMA   Harss, Luis and Barbara Dohmann
       Into the mainstream; conversations with
         Latin-American writers.
       New York, Harper, 1967.

INPO   Van Doren, Mark
       Introduction to poetry; commentaries on thirty
         poems.
       New York, Hill & Wang, 1966.

INTE   Littlejohn, David
       Interruptions.
       New York, Grossman Pubs., 1970.

IOGE   Jacobsen, Josephine and William R. Mueller
       Ionesco and Genet, playwrights of silence.
       New York, Hill & Wang, 1968.

JOJC   Cunningham, J. V.
       The journal of John Cardan.
       Denver, Alan Swallow, 1964.

JUPE   Juvenal
       Juvenal and Persius.
       Cambridge, Harvard Univ. Press, 1940.

JUSI   Fellini, Federico
       Juliet of the spirits.
       New York, Orion, 1965.

KAFK	Gray, Ronald, ed. Kafka; a collection of critical essays. Englewood Cliffs, N. J., Prentice-Hall, 1962.
KICA	Dupee, F. W. The king of the cats and other remarks on writers and writing. New York, Farrar, Straus, 1965.
LACL	Wilkinson, William Cleaver Latin Classics, v. 1. New York, Funk, 1900.
LAES	Mann, Thomas Last essays. New York, Knopf, 1958.
LAGL	Bowra, C. M. Landmarks in Greek literature. Cleveland, World Pub., 1966.
LANI	Baumbach, Jonathan The landscape of nightmare. New York, N. Y. Univ. Press, 1965.
LAPO	Guillen, Jorge Language and poetry; some poets of Spain. Cambridge, Harvard Univ. Press, 1961.
LAPR	Geismar, Maxwell The last of the provincials; the American novel, 1915-1925. Boston, Houghton, 1949.
LASA	Burke, Kenneth Language as symbolic action; essays on life, literature, and method. Berkeley, Univ. of Calif. Press, 1966.
LASI	Steiner, George Language and silence; essays on language, literature, and the inhuman. New York, Atheneum Pubs., 1967.
LASS	Rahv, Philip Literature and the sixth sense. Boston, Houghton, 1969.

LERB   Blair, Hugh
Lectures on rhetoric and belles lettres, v. 1.
Carbondale, Southern Ill. Univ. Press, 1965.

LERBL   Blair, Hugh
Lectures on rhetoric and belles lettres, v. 2.
Carbondale, Southern Ill. Univ. Press, 1965.

LIBN   Nyren, Dorothy, comp. and ed.
A library of literary criticism; Modern
    American literature.
New York, Ungar, 1964.

LICA   Knight, Everett W.
Literature considered as philosophy.
New York, Collier Bks., 1962.

LICR   Trilling, Lionel, ed.
Literary criticism; an introductory reader.
New York, Holt, 1970.

LIES   Daiches, David
Literary essays.
Chicago, Univ. of Chicago Press, 1956.

LIFD   Bentley, Eric
The life of the drama.
New York, Atheneum Pubs., 1964.

LIHA   Tyler, Moses Coit
The literary history of the American Revolu-
    tion, 1763-1783, v. 1: 1763-1776.
New York, Ungar, 1957.

LIHAR   Tyler, Moses Coit
The literary history of the American Revolu-
    tion, 1763-1783, v. 2: 1776-1783.
New York, Ungar, 1957.

LIHE   Baugh, Albert C., ed.
A literary history of England, 2nd ed.
New York, Appleton, 1967.

LIHI   Baugh, Albert C., ed.
A literary history of England, v. 1: The Mid-
    dle Ages, by Kemp Malone & Albert Baugh.
New York, Appleton, 1948.

LIHIA	Baugh, Albert C., ed. A literary history of England, v. 2: The Renaissance (1500-1660), by Tucker Brooke. New York, Appleton, 1948.
LIHIB	Baugh, Albert C., ed. A literary history of England, v. 3: The Restoration and Eighteenth Century (1660- 1789), by George Sherburn. New York, Appleton, 1948.
LIHIC	Baugh, Albert C., ed. A literary history of England, v. 4: The Nineteenth Century and after (1789-1939), by Samuel C. Chew. New York, Appleton, 1948.
LIHRO	Duff, J. Wight Literary history of Rome; from the origins to the close of the golden age. New York, Barnes & Noble, 1960.
LIHRS	Duff, J. Wight Literary history of Rome in the silver age. New York, Barnes & Noble, 1964.
LILC	Temple, Ruth Z. and Martin Tucker, comps. and eds. A library of literary criticism; modern British literature, v. 1: A-G. New York, Ungar, 1966.
LILI	Temple, Ruth Z. and Martin Tucker, comps. and eds. A library of literary criticism; modern British literature, v. 2: H-P. New York, Ungar, 1966.
LILIC	Temple, Ruth Z. and Martin Tucker, comps. and eds. A library of literary criticism; modern British literature, v. 3: Q-Z. New York, Ungar, 1966.
LINL	Pritchett, V. S. The living novel & later appreciations. New York, Random House, 1964.

LINO   Grossvogel, David
      Limits of the novel.
      Ithaca, N. Y., Cornell Univ. Press, 1968.

LIOA   Quinn, Arthur Hobson, ed.
      The literature of the American people: an
       historical and critical survey.
      New York, Appleton, 1951.

LIOS   Weinberg, Bernard
      The limits of symbolism; studies of five
       modern French poets.
      Chicago, Univ. of Chicago Press, 1966.

LIRE   Widmer, Kingsley
      The literary rebel.
      Carbondale, Southern Ill. Univ. Press, 1965.

LISH   Wimsatt, William K., Jr. & Cleanth Brooks
      Literary criticism; a short history.
      New York, Knopf, 1957.

LISI   Hassan, Ihab
      The literature of silence; Henry Miller and
       Samuel Beckett.
      New York, Knopf, 1967.

LISY   Tindall, William York
      The literary symbol.
      Bloomington, Ind. Univ. Press, 1955.

LITC   Suetonius Tranquillus, C.
      The lives of the twelve Caesars.
      New York, Modern Library, 1959.

LITR   Howard, Leon
      Literature and the American tradition.
      New York, Doubleday, 1960.

LIWM   Priestley, John B.
      Literature and western man.
      New York, Harper, 1960.

LODA   Fiedler, Leslie A.
      Love and death in the American novel.
      Cleveland, World Pub., 1960.

LUGD	Hall, James The lunatic giant in the drawing room; the British and American novel since 1930. Bloomington, Ind. Univ. Press, 1968.
LYCE	Camus, Albert Lyrical and critical essays. New York, Knopf, 1968.
MACA	Parrington, Vernon Louis Main currents in American thought. (3 v. in 1, individual pagination) New York, Harcourt, 1958.
MADE	Genet, Jean The maids and Deathwatch; two plays. New York, Grove, 1961.
MADR	Gassner, John Masters of the drama. New York, Dover Pub., 1954.
MAEN	Moravia, Alberto Man as an end; a defense of humanism. New York, Farrar, Straus, 1965.
MAIT	Podhoretz, Norman Making it. New York, Random House, 1967.
MALR	Wilkinson, David Malraux, an essay in political criticism. Cambridge, Harvard Univ. Press, 1967.
MAMF	Fuller, Edmund Man in modern fiction; some minority opinions in contemporary American writing. New York, Random House. 1958.
MAMI	Corrigan, Robert W., ed. Masterpieces of the modern Italian theatre. New York, Collier Bks., 1967.
MAMS	Corrigan, Robert W., ed. Masterpieces of the modern Spanish theatre. New York, Collier Bks., 1967.

179

MAPO   Untermeyer, Louis, ed.
              Modern American poetry.
              New York, Harcourt, 1958.

MARE   Mauriac, François
              A Mauriac reader.
              New York, Farrar, Straus, 1968.

MASM   Bewley, Marius
              Masks & mirrors.
              New York, Atheneum Pubs., 1970.

MATM   Rabinovich, Isaiah
              Major trends in modern Hebrew fiction.
              Chicago, Univ. of Chicago Press, 1968.

MAWH   Cowley, Malcolm
              A many-windowed house.
              Carbondale, Southern Ill. Univ. Press, 1970.

MERS   Lievsay, John L., ed.
              Medieval and Renaissance studies; proceedings
                  of the Southeastern Institute of Medieval and
                  Renaissance Studies, Summer, 1966.
              Durham, N. C., Duke Univ. Press, 1968.

META   Abel, Lionel
              Metatheatre.
              New York, Hill & Wang, 1963.

MIAN   Hoyt, Charles Alva, ed.
              Minor American novelists.
              Carbondale, Southern Ill. Univ. Press, 1970.

MICF   Fowlie, Wallace
              Mid-century French poets; selections, transla-
                  tions, and critical notices.
              New York, Twayne Pubs., 1955.

MIRO   O'Connor, Frank
              The mirror in the roadway; a study of the
                  modern novel.
              New York, Knopf, 1956.

MOAM   Mazzaro, Jerome, ed.
              Modern American poetry.
              New York, McKay, 1970.

MOAP	Gould, Jean Modern American playwrights. New York, Dodd, 1966.
MOBD	Brown, John Russell, ed. Modern British dramatists; a collection of critical essays. Englewood Cliffs, N. J., Prentice-Hall, 1968.
MOBF	Schorer, Mark, ed. Modern British fiction. New York, Oxford, 1961.
MODP	Hamilton, Ian, ed. The modern poet. New York, Horizon Press, 1968.
MOFT	Guicharnaud, Jacques Modern French theatre from Giraudoux to Beckett. New Haven, Yale Univ. Press, 1961.
MOIN	Vittorini, Domenico The modern Italian novel. New York, Russell & Russell, 1967.
MOMP	Southworth, James More modern American poets. Freeport, N. Y., Books for Libraries Press, 1954.
MONA	Hoffman, Frederick J. The modern novel in America. Chicago, Regnery, 1951.
MOPE	Hollander, John, ed. Modern poetry: essays in criticism. London, Oxford Univ. Press, 1968.
MOPO	Scully, James, ed. Modern poetics. New York, McGraw, 1965.
MOPR	Rosenthal, M. L. The modern poets; a critical introduction. New York, Oxford, 1960.

MOPW	Miller, J. William Modern playwrights at work, v. 1. New York, French, 1968.

MORL	Curley, Dorothy Nyren and Arthur Curley,
	    comps. and eds.
	A library of literary criticism: modern
	    Romance literatures.
	New York, Ungar, 1967.

MOTB	Ellman, Richard and Charles Fiedelson, eds. Modern tradition: backgrounds of modern literature. New York, Oxford, 1965.
MOWO	Hampshire, Stuart N. Modern writers and other essays. New York, Knopf, 1969.
MUFP	Haycraft, Howard Murder for pleasure; the life and times of the detective story. New York, Appleton, 1941.
MYPO	Rahv, Philip The myth and the powerhouse. New York, Farrar, Straus, 1965.
NAMA	Pirandello, Luigi Naked masks, five plays. New York, Dutton, 1952.
NASO	Margolies, Edward Native sons. Philadelphia, Lippincott, 1968.
NEDE	Neruda, Pablo A new decade (Poems: 1958-1967). New York, Grove, 1969.
NEFN	Le Sage, Laurent The new French novel. University Park, Pa. State Univ. Press, 1962.
NELI	Mauriac, Claude The new literature. New York, Braziller, 1959.

NENA   Weinberg, Helen
The new novel in America.
Ithaca, N. Y., Cornell Univ. Press, 1970.

NENO   Bone, Robert A.
The Negro novel in America.
New Haven, Yale Univ. Press, 1965.

NEVA   Gloster, Hugh M.
Negro voices in American fiction.
New York, Russell & Russell, 1948.

NEWP   Casper, Leonard
New writing from the Philippines.
Syracuse, Syracuse Univ. Press, 1966.

NEYT   Brown, Francis, ed.
Opinions and perspectives.
Boston, Houghton, 1964.

NIET   Aristotle
The Nicomachean ethics.
Cambridge, Harvard Univ. Press, 1934.

NOAM   Blake, Nelson Manfred
Novelists' America: fiction as history, 1910-
1940.
Syracuse, Syracuse Univ. Press, 1969.

NOFI   Bluestone, George
Novels into film.
Berkeley, Univ. of Calif. Press, 1966.

NOIT   Fiedler, Leslie
No! in thunder.
Boston, Beacon Press, 1960.

NOME   Davis, Robert Murray, ed.
The novel: modern essays in criticism.
Englewood Cliffs, N. J., Prentice-Hall, 1969.

NOMW   Daiches, David
The novel and the modern world. Rev. ed.
Chicago, Univ. of Chicago Press, 1960.

NOVA   Frohock, W. M.
The novel of violence in America.
Boston, Beacon Press, 1957.

NOVE   Drew, Elizabeth
            The novel.
            New York, Norton, 1963.

OBCO   Babbitt, Irving
            On being creative and other essays.
            New York, Biblo and Tannen, 1960.

OCDR   Dickinson, Thomas H.
            Outline of contemporary drama.
            New York, Houghton, 1927.

OCHI   Sachs, Nelly
            O the chimneys.
            New York, Farrar, Straus, 1967.

OCLI   Kostelanetz, Richard, ed.
            On contemporary literature.
            New York, Avon Bks., 1964.

ODPI   Pindar
            The odes of Pindar.
            Chicago, Univ. of Chicago Press, 1947.

ODYS   Kazantzakis, Nikos
            The odyssey, a modern sequel.
            New York, Simon & Schuster, 1958.

OJBO   Hackett, Francis
            On judging books; in general and in particular.
            New York, Day, 1947.

ONAC   Molière, Jean Baptiste Poquelin
            One-act comedies of Moliere.
            Cleveland, World Pub., 1964.

ONMU   Aristotle
            On man in the universe.
            New York, Walter J. Black, 1943.

OPPO   Eliot, T. S.
            On poetry and poets.
            New York, Farrar, Straus, 1957.

OPRI   Hayter, Alethea
            Opium and the romantic imagination.
            Berkeley, Univ. of Calif. Press, 1968.

OPSE	Trilling, Lionel The opposing self. New York, Viking, 1955.
ORUN	Donoghue, Denis The ordinary universe. New York, Macmillan, 1968.
OTIN	Borges, Jorge Luis Other inquisitions, 1937-1952. Austin, Univ. of Tex. Press, 1964.
OURL	Slonim, Marc An outline of Russian literature. New York, Oxford, 1958.
PAGO	Wilson, Edmund Patriotic gore. New York, Oxford, 1962.
PICA	Auchincloss, Louis Pioneers and caretakers. Minneapolis, Univ. of Minnesota Press, 1965.
PISA	Lewis, R. W. B. The picaresque saint. Philadelphia, Lippincott, 1958.
PLAC	Chekhov, Anton The plays of Anton Chekhov. New York, Caxton House, 1945.
PLDO	Frankenberg, Lloyd Pleasure dome: on reading modern poetry. New York, Gordian Press, 1949.
POAG	Jarrell, Randall Poetry and the age. New York, Vintage Bks., 1953.
POAR	Aristotle The politics of Aristotle. London, J. M. Dent, 1912.
POBF	Gindin, James Postwar British fiction. Berkeley, Univ. of Calif. Press, 1962.

POBL Levin, Harry
The power of blackness.
New York, Knopf, 1958.

POEX MacLeish, Archibald
Poetry and experience.
Boston, Houghton, 1960.

POHC Lewis, R. W. B.
Poetry of Hart Crane.
Princeton, Princeton Univ. Press, 1967.

POHU Vallejo, Cesar Abraham
Poemas humanos: human poems.
New York, Grove, 1968.

POLI Aristotle
Politics.
New York, Modern Library, 1943.

POMI Martz, Louis L.
The poem of the mind.
New York, Oxford, 1966.

PONN Rilke, Rainer Maria
Poems, 1906 to 1926.
New York, New Directions, 1957.

PONY Garcia Lorca, Federico
Poet in New York.
New York, Grove, 1955.

POOP Nemerov, Howard
Poets on poetry.
New York, Basic Bks., 1966.

POOT Deutsch, Babette
Poetry in our time.
New York, Columbia Univ. Press, 1956.

POPO Highet, Gilbert
Powers of poetry.
New York, Oxford, 1960.

POPP Pushkin, Alexander
The poems, prose and plays of Alexander
Pushkin.
New York, Modern Library, 1936.

POPR   Hungerford, Edward, ed.
      Poets in progress.
      Evanston, Northwestern Univ. Press, 1962.

PORE   Miller, Joseph Hillis
      Poets of reality.
      Cambridge, Harvard Univ. Press, 1965.

POSU   Kronenberger, Louis
      The polished surface.
      New York, Knopf, 1969.

POVO   Voltaire, François Marie Arouet de
      Portable Voltaire.
      New York, Viking, 1949.

POYY   Yevtushenko, Yevgeny
      Poetry of Yevgeny Yevtushenko, 1953 to 1965.
      New York, October House, 1965.

PRAB   Daiches, David
      The present age in British literature.
      Bloomington, Indiana Univ. Press, 1958.

PRTR   Brereton, Geoffrey
      Principles of tragedy.
      Coral Gables, Univ. of Miami Press, 1968.

PRVM   Mueller, William R.
      Prophetic voice in modern fiction.
      New York, Association Press, 1959.

PRWT   Madden, David, ed.
      Proletarian writers of the thirties.
      Carbondale, Southern Ill. Univ. Press, 1968.

PSLP   Crews, Frederick
      Psychoanalysis and literary process.
      Cambridge, Mass., Winthrop Pub., 1970.

PUPN   Stuckey, W. J.
      The Pulitzer prize novels.
      Norman, Univ. of Okla. Press, 1966.

RAIS   Hassan, Ihab
      Radical innocence: studies in the contemporary
        American novel.
      Princeton, Princeton Univ. Press, 1961.

RANU   Rideout, Walter B.
The radical novel in the United States, 1900-1954.
Cambridge, Harvard Univ. Press, 1956.

READ   Gagey, Edmond M.
Revolution in American drama.
New York, Columbia Univ. Press, 1947.

REAM   Ludwig, Jack
Recent American novelists.
Minneapolis, Univ. of Minn. Press, 1962.

REAN   Geismar, Maxwell
Rebels and ancestors.
Boston, Houghton, 1953.

REAP   Green, Martin
Re-appraisals: some commonsense readings in
American literature.
New York, Norton, 1965.

REDR   Miner, Earl, ed.
Restoration dramatists.
Englewood Cliffs, N. J., Prentice-Hall, 1966.

REHP   Grene, David
Reality and the heroic pattern.
Chicago, Univ. of Chicago Press, 1967.

REHV   Solotaroff, Theodore
The red hot vacuum.
New York, Atheneum Pubs., 1970.

REIM   Morgan, Charles
Reflections in a mirror.
New York, Macmillan, 1945.

REND   McCullough, Bruce
Representative English novelists: Defoe to
Conrad.
New York, Harper, 1946.

REVA   Fiedler, Leslie A.
Return of the vanishing American.
New York, Stein & Day, 1968.

188

RHGR   Clark, Donald Leman
            Rhetoric in Greco-Roman education.
            New York, Columbia Univ. Press, 1957.

RIAN   Cowie, Alexander
            The rise of the American novel.
            New York, American Book Co., 1951.

RICO   Rimbaud, Jean Nicolas Arthur
            Rimbaud complete works, selected letters.
            Chicago, Univ. of Chicago Press, 1966.

RIFA   Bier, Jesse
            The rise and fall of American humor.
            New York, Holt, 1968.

RIFM   Gross, John
            The rise and fall of the man of letters.
            New York, Macmillan, 1969.

RIFW   Taylor, John Russell
            The rise and fall of the well-made play.
            New York, Hill & Wang, 1967.

RINO   Watt, Ian
            The rise of the novel.
            Berkeley, Univ. of Calif. Press, 1967.

ROAG   Praz, Mario
            The romantic agony.
            New York, World, 1951.

ROAL   Halleck, Reuben Post
            The romance of American literature.
            New York, American Book Co., 1934.

RORH   Hahn, Emily
            Romantic rebels.
            Boston, Houghton, 1966.

RUNO   Reeve, F. D.
            The Russian novel.
            New York, McGraw, 1966.

RUOK   Omar Khayyam
            The Rubaiyat of Omar Khayyam.
            New York, Walter J. Black, 1942.

RUTH	Mihajlov, Mihajlo Russian themes. New York, Farrar, Straus, 1968.
SEES	Warren, Robert Penn Selected essays. New York, Random House, 1958.
SEHE	Rimbaud, Arthur A season in hell and the drunken boat. Norfolk, Conn., New Directions, 1961.
SELE	Lewis, C. S. Selected literary essays. Cambridge, Cambridge Univ. Press, 1969.
SELP	Yevtushenko, Yevgeny Selected poems. New York, Dutton, 1962.
SELW	Eluard, Paul Selected writings. Norfolk, Conn., New Directions.
SEMA	O'Connor, William Van, ed. Seven modern American novelists. Minneapolis, Univ. of Minn. Press, 1964.
SEPB	Brecht, Bertolt Seven plays by Bertolt Brecht. New York, Grove, 1961.
SEPL	Ghelderode, Michel de Seven plays. New York, Hill & Wang, 1960.
SEPM	Montale, Eugenio Selected poems. New York, New Directions, 1965.
SEPO	Mistral, Gabriela Selected poems of Gabriela Mistral. Bloomington, Indiana Univ. Press, 1957.
SEPP	Emerson, Ralph Waldo Selected prose and poetry. New York, Holt, 1950.

SEPR	Leopardi, Giacomo Selected prose and poetry. New York, New Am. Lib., 1966.
SEST	Weber, Brom, ed. Sense and sensibility in twentieth century writing. Carbondale, Southern Ill. Univ. Press, 1970.
SETO	Moskowitz, Sam Seekers of tomorrow. New York, World, 1966.
SEWB	Cendrars, Blaise Selected writings of Blaise Cendrars. New York, New Directions, 1966.
SEWJ	Jarry, Alfred Selected works. New York, Grove, 1965.
SEWO	Lucian Selected works. Indianapolis, Bobbs, 1965.
SEWR	Michaux, Henri Selected writings. New York, New Directions, 1951.
SEWS	Quasimodo, Salvatore. The selected writings of Salvatore Quasimodo. New York, Farrar, Straus, 1960.
SHAC	Ellison, Ralph Shadow and act. New York, Random House, 1964.
SHEL	Saintsbury, George Short history of English literature. London, Macmillan, 1964.
SHGO	Mooney, Harry S., Jr. and Thomas F. Staley, eds. The shapeless god. Pittsburgh, Univ. of Pittsburgh Press, 1968.

SHLI	Wilson, Edmund The shores of light. New York, Farrar, Straus, 1952.
SHRE	Wilson, Edmund, ed. The shock of recognition. New York, Farrar, Straus, 1955.
SHSE	Canby, Henry Seidel The short story in English. New York, Holt, 1909.
SODJ	Echegaray y Eizaguirre, Jose The son of Don Juan. Boston, Little, 1911.
SORL	Slonim, Marc Soviet Russian literature; writers and problems. New York, Oxford, 1964.
SPAL	Anderson-Imbert, Enrique Spanish American literature; a history. Detroit, Wayne State Univ. Press, 1963.
SPLE	Poggioli, Renato Spirit of the letter. Cambridge, Harvard Univ. Press, 1965.
SPTR	Muller, Herbert J. The spirit of tragedy. New York, Knopf, 1956.
STAN	Hyman, Stanley Edgar Standards: a chronicle of books for our time. New York, Horizon Press, 1966.
STCA	Lawrence, D. H. Studies in classic American literature. New York, Viking, 1961.
STCL	Pearce, Richard Stages of the clown. Carbondale, Southern Ill. Univ. Press, 1970.

STHT   Poulet, Georges
Studies in human time.
Baltimore, John Hopkins Press, 1956.

SYPO   Engelberg, Edward, ed.
Symbolist poem.
New York, Dutton, 1967.

TEAH   Morris, Wright
The territory ahead.
New York, Atheneum Pubs., 1963.

TEEX   Cioran, Emile M.
The temptation to exist.
Chicago, Quadrangle Bks., 1968.

TEFV   Villon, François
The testaments of François Villon.
New York, Liveright Pub., 1924.

THAB   Esslin, Martin
Theatre of the absurd.
Garden City, N. Y., Doubleday, 1961.

THBU   Cowley, Malcolm
Think back on us...
Carbondale, Southern Ill. Univ. Press, 1967.

THPL   Giraudoux, Jean
Three plays: Judith; tiger at the gates; duel
     of angels.
New York, Oxford, 1963.

THPP   Wellwarth, George
Theatre of protest and paradox.
New York, N. Y. Univ. Press, 1964.

TILI   Rascoe, Burton
Titans of literature.
New York, Putnam, 1932.

TIMW   Brooks, Van Wyck
The times of Melville and Whitman.
New York, Dutton, 1947.

TIPI   Raleigh, John Henry
Time, place, and idea.
Carbondale, Southern Ill. Univ. Press, 1968.

TOCC	Eliot, T. S. To criticize the critic and other writings. New York, Farrar, Straus, 1965.
TOCN	Pirandello, Luigi To clothe the naked, and two other plays. New York, Dutton, 1962.
TOGW	Madden, David, ed. Tough guy writers of the thirties. Carbondale, Southern Ill. Univ. Press, 1968.
TRTH	Wilson, Edmund Triple thinkers: twelve essays on literary subjects. New York, Oxford, 1948.
TRWO	Lewis, R. W. B. Trials of the word. New Haven, Yale Univ. Press, 1965.
TWDR	Moers, Ellen Two Dreisers. New York, Viking, 1969.
TWEN	Hoffman, Frederick J. The Twenties. Rev. ed. New York, Free Press, 1962.
TWGA	Mizener, Arthur Twelve great American novels. New York, New Am. Lib., 1967.
TWPO	Neruda, Pablo Twenty poems. Madison, Minn., The Sixties Press, 1967.
UGBE	Betti, Ugo Ugo Betti: three plays. New York, Hill & Wang, 1966.
VAHE	O'Faolain, Sean The vanishing hero. Boston, Little, 1957.

VIDE	Chapman, Raymond Victorian debate New York, Basic Bks., 1968.
VILA	Smith, Henry Nash Virgin land. New York, Vintage Bks., 1950.
VILI	Preyer, Robert O., ed. Victorian literature. New York, Harper, 1967.
VINO	Cecil, David Victorian novelists. Chicago, Univ. of Chicago Press, 1958.
VINU	Dante Alighieri La vita nuova. Bloomington, Ind. Univ. Press, 1962.
VOSN	Carlisle, Olga Andreyev Voices in the snow. New York, Random House, 1962.
WAFE	Fiedler, Leslie A. Waiting for the end. New York, Stein & Day, 1964.
WEWU	Brooks, Cleanth The well wrought urn. New York, Harcourt, 1947.
WHIF	Tucholsky, Kurt What if--? New York, Funk, 1967.
WHNO	Gide, Andre The white notebook. New York, Citadel, 1965.
WIFT	Thompson, Lawrance William Faulkner. New York, Barnes & Noble, 1963.
WIHO	Auslander, Joseph and Frank Ernest Hill Winged horse. New York, Doubleday, 1955.

WITS	Troy, William William Troy: selected essays. New Brunswick, N. J., Rutgers Univ. Press, 1967.
WOBO	Wilson, Edmund The wound and the bow. New York, Oxford, 1941.
WOEL	Poirier, Richard A world elsewhere. New York, Oxford Univ. Press, 1956.
WOMM	Moliere, Jean-Baptiste Poquelin The works of Monsieur de Moliere, v. 1. New York, Benjamin Blom, Inc., 1967.
WOPL	Plato The works of Plato. New York, Modern Library, 1928.
WOVN	Marshall, William H. The world of the Victorian novel. South Brunswick, N. J., A. S. Barnes, 1967.
WOWE	Schorer, Mark World we imagine. New York, Farrar, Straus, 1968.
WOWI	Brooks, Van Wyck The world of Washington Irving. New York, Dutton, 1944.
WRIC	Geismar, Maxwell Writers in crisis. Boston, Houghton, 1961.
WRIR	Seaver, Richard, ed. Writers in revolt. New York, Frederick Fell, 1963.
WROW	McCarthy, Mary The writing on the wall... New York, Harcourt, 1970.

WRWC   Hildeck, Wallace
Writing with care.
New York, David White, 1967.

WWFS   Paris Review (The)
Writers at work (first series).
New York, Viking, 1958.

WWSS   Paris Review (The)
Writers at work (second series).
New York, Viking, 1963.

WWTS   Paris Review (The)
Writers at work (third series).
New York, Viking, 1967.

YILI   Madison, Charles A.
Yiddish literature.
New York, Ungar, 1968.

AUTHOR INDEX TO BOOKS ANALYZED

Abel, Lionel, <u>Metatheatre</u>.   META

Adereth, M., <u>Commitment in modern French</u>.   COMF

Albert, Edward, <u>A history of English literature</u>.   HIEL

Alexandrova, Vera, <u>A history of Soviet literature</u>.   HISL

Allen, Everett S., <u>Famous American humorous poets</u>.   FAAH

Alter, Robert, <u>After the tradition</u>.   AFTR

<u>The American literary anthology, v. 1</u>.   AMLA

<u>The American literary anthology, v. 2</u>.   AMLI

Anderson-Imbert, Enrique, <u>Spanish American literature</u>.   SPAL

Aristophanes, <u>The eleven comedies</u>.   ELCO

Aristotle, <u>Aristotle: selections</u>.   ARIS

_____, <u>The basic works of Aristotle</u>.   BAWA

_____, <u>Introduction to Aristotle</u>.   INAR

_____, <u>The Nicomachean ethics</u>.   NIET

_____, <u>On man in the universe</u>.   ONMU

_____, <u>Politics</u>.   POLI

_____, <u>The politics of Aristotle</u>.   POÁR

Auchincloss, Louis, <u>Pioneers and caretakers</u>.   PICA

Auslander, Joseph and Frank Ernest Hill,
Winged horse.   WIHO

Babbitt, Irving, On being creative and other essays. OBCO

Balakian, Nona and Charles Simmons, eds. The
creative present.   CRPR

Baugh, Albert C., ed., A literary History of
England   LIHE

_____, A literary history of England, v. 1.   LIHI

_____, A literary history of England, v. 2.   LIHIA

_____, A literary history ofEngland, v. 3.   LIHIB

_____, A literary history of England, v. 4.   LIHIC

Baumbach, Jonathan, The landscape of nightmare. LANI

Beach, Joseph Warren, American fiction, 1920-1940. AMFI

Benjamin, Walter, Illuminations.   ILLU

Bentley, Eric, ed., Importance of Scrutiny.   IMSC

_____, The life of the drama.   LIFD

Bergonzi, Bernard, Heroes' twilight.   HERT

Berthoff, Warner, The ferment of realism.   FERE

Bertocci, Angelo Philip, From symbolism to
Baudelaire.   FRSB

Betti, Ugo, Ugo Betti: three plays.   UGBE

Bewley, Marius, Masks & mirrors.   MASM

Bier, Jesse, The rise and fall of American humor. RIFA

Bigsby, C. W. E., ed., The black American writer,
v. 1.   BLAW

_____, The black American writer, v. 2.   BLAWP

Blackmur, R. P., The double agent.   DAEC

Blair, Hugh, Lectures on rhetoric and belles lettres,
   v. 1.   LERB

_____, Lectures on rhetoric and belles lettres,
   v. 2.   LERBL

Blake, Nelson Manfred, Novelists' America.   NOAM

Bluestone, George, Novels into film.   NOFI

Bone, Robert A., The Negro novel in America.   NENO

Borges, Jorge Luis, Dreamtigers.   DREA

_____, Other inquisitions, 1937-1952.   OTIN

Bowra, C. M., Landmarks in Greek literature.   LAGL

Brecht, Bertolt, Seven plays by Bertolt Brecht.   SEPB

Brereton, Geoffrey, Principles of tragedy.   PRTR

Brieux, Eugene, Blanchette and the escape...   BLES

Brooks, Cleanth, The well wrought urn.   WEWU

Brooks, Van Wyck, The confident years: 1885-1915. COYE

_____, The flowering of New England.   FLNE

_____, The times of Melville and Whitman.   TIMW

_____, The world of Washington Irving.   WOWI

Brown, Francis, ed., Opinions and perspectives.   NEYT

Brown, John Russell, ed., Modern British dramatists.
                                        MOBD

Bryer, Jackson R., Fifteen modern American
   authors.   FIMA

Buckley, Vincent. Essays in poetry, mainly
   Australian.   ESPO

Buckman, Thomas R., ed., Bibliography and
natural history.   BINA

Buonarroti Michelangelo, Complete poems and
selected letters of Michelangelo.   COPS

Burke, Kenneth, Language as symbolic action.   LASA

Caesar, Caius Julius, The Gallic War and other
writings.   GAWA

Camus, Albert, Lyrical and critical essays.   LYCE

Canby, Henry Seidel, The short story in English.   SHSE

Carlisle, Olga Andreyev, Voices in the snow.   VOSN

Casona, Alejandro, La barca sin pescador.   BASP

Casper, Leonard, New writing from the Philippines. NEWP

Cecil, David, Victorian novelists.   VINO

Cendrars, Blaise, Selected writings of Blaise
Cendrars.   SEWB

Chandler, Alice, A dream of order.   DROR

Chapman, Raymond, Victorian debate.   VIDE

Charlesworth, Barbara, Dark passages.   DAPA

Chekhov, Anton, The plays of Anton Chekhov.   PLAC

Chiari, Joseph, Contemporary French poetry.   COFP

Cicero, Marcus Tullius, The basic works of Cicero. BAWC

Cioran, Emile M.   The temptation to exist.   TEEX

Clark, Donald Leman, Rhetoric in Greco-Roman
education.   RHGR

Cohen, Arthur A., Arguments and doctrines.   ARDO

Cohen, J. M., A history of western literature.   HIWL

Corneille, Pierre, The chief plays of Corneille.   CHPC

Corrigan, Robert W., ed., Masterpieces of the
    modern Italian theatre.   MAMI

_____, Masterpieces of the modern Spanish
theatre.   MAMS

Cowie, Alexander, The rise of the American novel.   RIAN

Cowley, Malcolm, ed., After the genteel tradition.   AFGT

_____, Exile's return.   EXRE

_____, A many-windowed house.   MAWH

_____, Think back on us...   THBU

Crews, Frederick, Psychoanalysis and literary
    process.   PSLP

Cunliffe, J. W., English literature in the twentieth
    century.   ENLT

Cunningham, J. V., The journal of John Cardan.   JOJC

Curley, Dorothy Nyren and Arthur Curley, comps. and eds.
    A library of literary criticism.   MORL

Curtis, C. J., Contemporary Protestant thought.   COPT

Daiches, David, Critical approaches to literature.   CRAL

_____, Literary essays.   LIES

_____, The novel and the modern world.   NOMW

_____, The present age in British literature.   PRAB

Dante Alighieri, The divine comedy.   DICO

_____, The divine comedy, v. 3 & 4.   DIVC

_____, La vita nuova.   VINU

Davis, Robert Murray, ed., The novel.   NOME

Davis, Ruth, The great books of Russia.　　GRBR

Davis, Walter R., Idea and act in Elizabethan
　fiction.　　IDAE

Deutsch, Babette, Poetry in our time.　　POOT

Dickey, James, Babel to Byzantium.　　BABY

Dickinson, Thomas H., Outline of contemporary
　drama.　　OCDR

Donoghue, Denis, Connoisseurs of chaos.　　COCH

　―――――――. The ordinary universe.　　ORUN

Downs, Robert B., Books that changed America.　　BOTC

Drew, Elizabeth, The novel.　　NOVE

Duckworth, George E., ed., The complete Roman
　drama, v. 1.　　CORD

Duff, J. Wight, The literary history of Rome.　　LIHRO

　―――――――. Literary history of Rome in the
　silver age.　　LIHRS

Dupee, F. W., King of the cats.　　KICA

Durant, Will and Ariel Durant, Interpretations of
　life.　　INLI

Echegaray y Eizaguirre, José, The son of Don Juan. SODJ

Edgar, Pelham, The art of the novel.　　ARNO

Eisinger, Chester E., Fiction of the forties.　　FIFO

Eliot, T. S., On poetry and poets.　　OPPO

　―――――――. To criticize the critic and other
　writings.　　TOCC

Ellison, Ralph, Shadow and act.　　SHAC

Ellman, Richard and Charles Feidelson, eds.,
　Modern tradition.　　MOTB

204

Eluard, Paul, Selected writings.   SELW

Emerson, Ralph Waldo, Selected prose and poetry.   SEPP

Engelberg, Edward, ed., Symbolist poem.   SYPO

English Institute, Experience in the novel.   EXNO

Epictetus, The discourses of Epictetus.   DIEP

Era of Goethe.   ERGO

Esslin, Martin, Theatre of the absurd.   THAB

Evergreen Review, Evergreen Review reader.   EVRR

Fellini, Federico, Juliet of the spirits.   JUSI

Fiedler, Leslie A., Love and death in the American
     novel.   LODA

_____, No! in thunder.   NOIT

_____, Return of the vanishing American.   REVA

_____, Waiting for the end.   WAFE

Forster, E. M., Aspects of the novel.   ASPN

Fowlie, Wallace, Andre Gide: his life and art.   ANGH

_____, The clown's grail.   CLGR

_____, Dionysus in Paris.   DIPA

_____, Guide to contemporary French literature.   GUCF

_____, Mid-century French poets.   MICF

Frankenberg, Lloyd, Pleasure dome.   PLDO

Frohock, W. M., The novel of violence in America.   NOVA

Fuller, Edmund, Man in modern fiction.   MAMF

Fussell, Edwin, Frontier.   FRAL

Gagey, Edmond M., Revolution in American drama.　READ

Garcia Lorca, Federico, The gypsy ballads of Federico Garcia Lorca.　GYBA

_____, Poet in New York.　PONY

Gardiner, Harold C., Fifty years of the American novel.　FIYA

Garland, Hamlin, Crumbling idols.　CRID

Gassner, John, Masters of the drama.　MADR

Geismar, Maxwell, American moderns.　AMMO

_____, The last of the provincials.　LAPR

_____, Rebels and ancestors.　REAN

_____, Writers in crisis.　WRIC

Genet, Jean, The maids and Deathwatch.　MADE

Ghelderode, Michel de, Seven plays, v. 1.　SEPL

Gide, Andre, The white notebook.　WHNO

Gillie, Christopher, Character in English literature.　CHEL

Gilman, Richard, The confusion of realms.　CONR

Gindin, James, Postwar British fiction.　POBF

Giraudoux, Jean, Three plays.　THPL

Gloster, Hugh M., Negro voices in American fiction.　NEVA

Goethe, Johann Wolfgang von, Goethe's Faust.　GOFA

Goldhurst, William, F. Scott Fitzgerald and his contemporaries.　FSFH

Gould, Jean, Modern American playwrights.　MOAP

Gray, Ronald, ed., Kafka; a collection of critical essays.　KAFK

Green, Martin, Re-appraisals.   REAP

Gregory, Horace and Marya Zaturenska, History of
    American poetry.   HIAP

Grene, David, Reality and the heroic pattern.   REHP

Gross, John, The rise and fall of the man of
    letters.   RIFM

Grossvogel, David I., Four playwrights and a
    postscript.   FOPP

_____, Limits of the novel.   LINO

Guicharnaud, Jacques, Modern French theatre from
    Giraudoux to Beckett.   MOFT

Guillen, Jorge, Cantico.   CANT

_____, Language and poetry.   LAPO

Hackett, Francis, On judging books.   OJBO

Hadas, Moses, Ancilla to classical reading.   ANCR

_____, A history of Greek literature.   HIGR

_____, A history of Latin literature.   HILL

Hahn, Emily, Romantic rebels.   RORH

Hall, James, Lunatic giant in the drawing room.   LUGD

Halleck, Reuben Post, The romance of American
    literature.   ROAL

Hamburger, Kate, From Sophocles to Sartre.   FRSS

Hamburger, Michael, Contraries.   COSG

Hamilton, Edith, The echo of Greece.   ECGR

_____, The ever present past.   EVPP

_____, The Greek way.   GRWA

Hamilton, Ian, ed., The modern poet.   MODP

Hampshire, Stuart N., Modern writers and other
essays.   MOWO

Harss, Luis and Barbara Dohmann, Into the main-
stream.   INMA

Hassan, Ihab, The literature of silence.   LISI

_____. Radical innocence.   RAIS

Haycraft, Howard, Murder for pleasure.   MUFP

Hayter, Alethea, Opium and the romantic
imagination.   OPRI

Highet, Gilbert, Powers of poetry.   POPO

Hildeck, Wallace, Writing with care.   WRWC

Hoffman, Frederick J., The modern novel in
America.   MONA

_____, The twenties.   TWEN

Holland, Norman N., The first modern comedies.   FIMC

Hollander, John, ed., Modern poetry.   MOPE

Howard, Leon, Literature and the American tradition. LITR

Howard, Richard, Alone with America.   ALWA

Howe, Irving, Decline of the new.   DENE

Hoyt, Charles Alva, ed., Minor American novelists. MIAN

Hungerford, Edward, ed., Poets in progress.   POPR

Hyman, Stanley Edgar, Standards.   STAN

Jacobsen, Josephine and William R. Mueller,
Ionesco and Genet, playwrights of silence.   IOGE

Jarrell, Randall, Poetry and the age.   POAG

Jarry, Alfred, Selected works.   SEWJ

Jones, Howard Mumford, <u>Belief and disbelief in American literature.</u>   BEDA

Juvenal, <u>Juvenal and Persius.</u>   JUPE

Karl, Frederick R., <u>An age of fiction.</u>   AGFI

_____, <u>The contemporary English novel.</u>   CONE

Kazantzakis, Nikos, <u>The odyssey.</u>   ODYS

Kazin, Alfred, <u>Contemporaries.</u>   CONT

Kenner, Hugh, <u>Flaubert, Joyce and Beckett.</u>   FLJB

Kermode, Frank, <u>Continuities.</u>   CONTI

Kettle, Arnold, <u>An introduction to the English novel, v. 1.</u>   INEN

_____, <u>An introduction to the English novel, v. 2.</u>   INENO

Knight, Everett W., <u>Literature considered as philosophy.</u>   LICA

Kostelanetz, Richard, ed., <u>On contemporary literature.</u>   OCLI

Kronenberger, Louis, <u>The polished surface.</u>   POSU

Krutch, Joseph Wood, <u>American drama since 1918.</u>   AMDR

Kumar, Shiv K., ed., <u>British Victorian literature.</u>   BRVL

Lawall, Sarah N., <u>Critics of consciousness.</u>   CRCO

Lawrence, D. H., <u>Studies in classic American literature.</u>   STCA

Leavis, F. R., <u>The great tradition.</u>   GRTR

Lee, Robert Edson, <u>From West to East.</u>   FRWE

Leopardi, Giacomo, <u>Selected prose and poetry.</u>   SEPR

Le Sage, Laurent, <u>The new French novel.</u>   NEFN

Lesky, Albin, A history of Greek literature. HIGL

Levin, Harry, The power of blackness. POBL

Lewis, Allan, American plays and playwrights of the contemporary theatre. AMPL

Lewis, Allan, The contemporary theatre. COTH

Lewis, C. S., Selected literary essays. SELE

Lewis, R. W. B., The picaresque saint. PISA

_____, Poetry of Hart Crane. POHC

_____, Trials of the word. TRWO

Lievsay, John L., ed., Medieval and Renaissance studies. MERS

Littlejohn, David, Interruptions. INTE

Lowell, James Russell, Complete poetical works of John Russell Lowell. COPW

Lucian, Selected works. SEWO

Ludwig, Jack, Recent American novelists. REAM

McCarthy, Mary, Writing on the wall... WROW

McCormack, Thomas, comp., Afterwords. AFTE

McCullough, Bruce, Representative English novelists. REND

MacLeish, Archibald, Poetry and experience. POEX

McLuhan, Marshall, The interior landscape. INLA

Madden, David, ed., American dreams, American nightmares. AMDA

_____, Proletarian writers of the thirties. PRWT

_____, Tough guy writers of the thirties. TOGW

Madison, Charles A., Yiddish literature. YILI

Malin, Irving and Irwin Stark, Breakthrough. BREA

Mandel, Siegfried, ed., Contemporary European
novelists. COEN

Mann, Thomas, Essays of three decades. ESTD

_____, Last essays. LAES

Margolies, Edward, Native sons. NASO

Marshall, William H., The world of the Victorian
novel. WOVN

Martz, Louis L., The poem of the mind. POMI

Matthiessen, F. O., American renaissance. AMRE

Maugham, W. Somerset, The art of fiction. ARFI

Mauriac, Claude, The new literature. NELI

Mauriac, François, A Mauriac reader. MARE

Maurois, Andre, From Proust to Camus. FRPC

Mazzaro, Jerome, ed., Modern American poetry. MOAM

Michaux, Henri, Selected writings. SEWR

Mihajlov, Mihajlo, Russian themes. RUTH

Miller, Henry, The books in my life. BOML

Miller, J. William, Modern playwrights at work,
v. 1. MOPW

Miller, Joseph Hillis, Poets of reality. PORE

Miller, Liam, The Dolmen Press Yeats centenary
papers. DOPY

Mills, Ralph J., Jr., Contemporary American
poetry. COAP

Miner, Earl, ed., Restoration dramatists. REDR

Mistral, Gabriela, Selected poems of Gabriela Mistral. SEPO

Mizener, Arthur. Twelve great American novels. TWGA

Moers, Ellen, Two Dreisers. TWDR

Moliere, Jean Baptiste Poquelin, One act comedies
of Moliere. ONAC

_____, The works of Monsieur de Moliere, v. 1. WOMM

Montale, Eugenio, Selected poems. SEPM

Mooney, Harry S., Jr. and Thomas F. Staley, eds.,
The shapeless god. SHGO

Moore, Harry T., ed., Contemporary American
novelists. COAN

Moravia, Alberto, Man as an end. MAEN

Morgan, Charles, Reflections in a mirror. REIM

Morris, Wright, The territory ahead. TEAH

Moskowitz, Sam, Explorers of the infinite. EXIN

_____. Seekers of tomorrow. SETO

Mueller, William R., Prophetic voice in modern
fiction. PRVM

Muller, Herbert J., The spirit of tragedy. SPTR

Munk, Kaj, Five plays. FIPL

Natan, Alex, ed., Essays on contemporary German
literature, v. 4. GEML

Nemerov, Howard, Poets on poetry. POOP

Neruda, Pablo, A new decade. NEDE

_____, Twenty poems. TWPO

_____, Heights of Macchu Picchu. HEMP

Noble, David W., The eternal Adam and the new
world garden. ETAN

Nyren, Dorothy, comp. and ed., A library of
  literary criticism.   LIBN

O'Brien, Justin, The French literary horizon.   FRLH

O'Connor, Frank, The mirror in the roadway.   MIRO

O'Connor, William Van, ed., Seven modern American
  novelists.   SEMA

O'Faolain, Sean, The vanishing hero.   VAHE

Omar Khayyam, The Rubaiyat of Omar Khayyam.   RUOK

Orwell, George, Collected essays..., vol. 1.   COEA

_____, Collected essays..., vol. 2.   COEB

_____, Collected essays..., vol. 3.   COEC

_____, Collected essays..., vol. 4.   COED

Pacifici, Sergio, A guide to contemporary Italian
  literature.   GUCI

Paris Review, Writers at work, first series.   WWFS

_____, Writers at work, second series.   WWSS

_____, Writers at work, third series.   WWTS

Parrington, Vernon Louis, Main currents in
  American thought.   MACA

Pascal, Roy, The German novel.   GENO

Pattee, Fred Lewis, The development of the
  American short story.   DEAS

Pearce, Richard. Stages of the clown.   STCL

Peden, William, The American short story.   AMSS

Peguy, Charles, Basic verities.   BAVE

Perez Galdos, Benito, Dona Perfecto.   DOPE

Perry, Bliss, American spirit in literature.   AMSL

Peyre, Henri, ed., Fiction in several languages. FISL

Phelps, William Lyon, Essays on Russian novelists. ESRN

Pindar, The odes of Pindar. ODPI

Pirandello, Luigi, Naked masks. NAMA

_____, To clothe the naked, and two other plays. TOCN

Plato, The works of Plato. WOPL

Podhoretz, Norman, Making it. MAIT

Poggioli, Renato, Spirit of the letter. SPLE

Poirier, Richard, A world elsewhere. WOEL

Porter, Katherine Anne, Collected essays and
occasional writings... CEOW

Poulet, Georges, Studies in human time. STHT

Powell, Lawrence Clark, Bookman's progress. BPSW

_____, California classics: the creative literature
of the golden state. CACL

Praz, Mario, The romantic agony. ROAG

Preyer, Robert O., ed., Victorian literature. VILI

Priestley, J. B., Essays of five decades. ESFI

_____, Literature and western man. LIWM

Pritchett, V. S., The living novel & later
appreciations. LINL

Pushkin, Alexander, Eugene Onegin, v. 3. EUON

_____, The poems, prose and plays of Alexander
Pushkin. POPP

Quasimodo, Salvatore, The selected writings of
Salvatore Quasimodo. SEWS

Quinn, Arthur Hobson, American fiction.　　　AMFH

_____, A history of the American drama from the beginning to the Civil War.　　　HIAM

_____, A history of the American drama from the Civil War to the present day.　　　HIAD

_____, The literature of the American people.　　　LIOA

Rabelais, François, The five books of Gargantua.　　　FIBG

Rabinovich, Isaiah, Major trends in modern Hebrew fiction.　　　MATM

Racine, Jean, The best plays of Racine.　　　BEPR

Rahv, Philip, Literature and the sixth sense.　　　LASS

_____, The myth and the powerhouse.　　　MYPO

Raleigh, John Henry, Time, place, and idea.　　　TIPI

Rascoe, Burton, Titans of literature.　　　TILI

Reeve, F. D., The Russian novel.　　　RUNO

Rexroth, Kenneth, Classics revisited.　　　CLRE

Richardson, Lyon N., Henry James.　　　HENR

Rideout, Walter B., The radical novel in the United States.　　　RANU

Rilke, Rainer Maria, Poems, 1906 to 1926.　　　PONN

Rimbaud, Jean Nicolas Arthur, Rimbaud complete works, selected letters.　　　RICO

_____, A season in hell and the drunken boat.　　　SEHE

Robbe-Grillet, Alain, For a new novel.　　　FONN

Rose, Ernst, A history of German literature.　　　HIGE

Rosenthal, M. L., The modern poets.　　　MOPR

Rourke, Constance, American humor.　　　AMHU

Ruiz, Juan, The book of good love.   BOGL

Sachs, Nelly, O the chimneys.   OCHI

Saintsbury, George, A history of criticism and
literary taste in Europe, v. 1.   HICL

_____, A history of criticism and literary taste
in Europe, v. 2.   HICR

_____, A history of criticism and literary taste
in Europe, v. 3.   HICT

_____, A short history of English literature.   SHEL

Scholes, Robert, Elements of fiction.   ELFI

_____, The fabulators.   FABU

Schorer, Mark, ed., Modern British fiction.   MOBF

_____, World we imagine.   WOWE

Scully, James, ed., Modern poetics.   MOPO

Seaver, Richard, ed., Writers in revolt.   WRIR

Shapiro, Karl, In defense of ignorance.   INDI

Slonim, Marc, An outline of Russian literature.   OURL

_____, Soviet Russian literature.   SORL

Smith, Henry Nash, Virgin land.   VILA

Smith, James, Harry and Edd Winfield Parks, ed.,
The great critics.   GRCR

Solotaroff, Theodore, The red hot vacuum.   REHV

Sontag, Susan, Against interpretation and other
essays.   AGIN

Southworth, James, More modern American poets. MOMP

Spiller, Robert E., The cycle of American literature.
        CYAL

Springhorn, Evert, ed., The genius of the Scandinavian theater. GESC

Starkie, Walter, tr., Eight Spanish plays of the golden age. EISP

Steeves, Harrison R., Before Jane Austen... BEJA

Stegner, Wallace, ed., American novel. AMNF

Steiner, George, The death of tragedy. DETR

_____, Language and silence. LASI

Stepanchev, Stephen, American poetry since 1945. AMPO

Stuckey, W. J., The Pulitzer prize novels. PUPN

Suetonius Tranquillus, C., The lives of the twelve Caesars. LITC

Tacitus, Cornelius, The complete works of Tacitus. COWO

Tate, Allen, Essays of four decades. ESFD

Taylor, John Russell, The angry theatre. ANTH

_____, The rise and fall of the well-made play. RIFW

Temple, Ruth Z. and Martin Tucker, comps. and eds., A library of literary criticism, v. 1. LILC

_____, A library of literary criticism, v. 2. LILI

_____, A library of literary criticism, v. 3. LILIC

Thibaudet, Albert, French literature from 1795 to our era. FRLI

Thompson, Lawrance, William Faulkner. WIFT

Thorp, William W., American writing in the twentieth century. AWTC

Thucydides, The complete writings of Thucydides. COWT

Tillyard, E. M., The English epic and its background. ENEI

Tindall, William York, The literary symbol.　　　LISY

Torres Rioseco, Arturo, The epic of Latin American
　literature.　　　EPLA

Trilling, Lionel, Beyond culture.　　　BEYC

＿＿＿＿＿, ed., Literary criticism.　　　LICR

＿＿＿＿＿, The opposing self.　　　OPSE

Troy, William, William Troy: selected essays.　　　WITS

Tucholsky, Kurt, What if--?　　　WHIF

Tuckerman, Frederick Goddard, Complete poems of
　Frederick Goddard Tuckerman.　　　COPF

Tyler, Moses Coit, The literary history of the
　American Revolution, v. 1.　　　LIHA

＿＿＿＿＿, The literary history of the American
　Revolution, v. 2.　　　LIHAR

Unterecker, John, ed., Approaches to the twentieth-
　century novel.　　　APTC

Untermeyer, Louis, ed., Modern American poetry.　MAPO

Updike, John, Assorted prose.　　　ASPR

Vallejo, Cesar Abraham, Poemas humanos.　　　POHU

Van Doren, Carl and Mark Van Doren, American
　and British literature since 1890.　　　AMBL

Van Doren, Carl, The American novel, 1789-1939.　AMNO

＿＿＿＿＿, Contemporary American novelists, 1900-
　1920.　　　COAM

Van Doren, Mark, The happy critic and other essays.
　　　HACR

＿＿＿＿＿, Introduction to poetry.　　　INPO

Van Ghent, Dorothy, The English novel.　　　ENNO

Van Nostrand, A. D., Everyman his own poet.   EVHO

Villas, James, Gerard de Nerval.   GEDN

Villon, François, The complete works of François Villon.   COWF

_____, The testaments of François Villon.   TEFV

Vittorini, Domenico, The modern Italian novel.   MOIN

Vogel, Stanley M., ed., An outline of American literature, v. 1.   COOC

Voltaire, Francois Marie Arouet de, Candide and other writings.   CAOW

_____, Portable Voltaire.   POVO

Voznesensky, Andrei, Antiworlds.   ANTI

_____, Antiworlds and the fifth ace.   ANFC

Wagenknecht, Edward, Cavalcade of the American novel.   CAAN

_____, Cavalcade of the English novel.   CAEN

Waggoner, Hyatt, H., American poets from the Puritans to the present.   AMPP

Wallace, Irving, The fabulous originals.   FAOR

Warren, Robert Penn, Selected essays.   SEES

Watt, Ian, The rise of the novel.   RINO

Weales, Gerald, American drama since World War II.   AMDS

Weber, Brom, ed., Sense and sensibility in twentieth century writing.   SEST

Weinberg, Bernard, The limits of symbolism.   LIOS

Weinberg, Helen, The new novel in America.   NENA

Wellek, Rene, A history of modern criticism, v. 1.   HIMC

_____, A history of modern criticism, v. 2.   HIMW

_____, A history of modern criticism, v. 3.   HIOC

_____, A history of modern criticism, v. 4.   HIOM

Wellwarth, George, Theatre of protest and paradox.   THPP

Wescott, Glenway, Images of truth.   IMTR

Whittier, John Greenleaf, Complete poetical works...   COPO

Widmer, Kingsley, The literary rebel.   LIRE

Wilkins, Ernest Hatch, A history of Italian literature.   HIIL

Wilkinson, David, Malraux, an essay in political
    criticism.   MALR

Wilkinson, William Cleaver, Latin classics, v. 1.   LACL

Wilson, Edmund, Axel's castle.   AXCA

_____, The bit between my teeth.   BIBM

_____, Classics and commercials.   CLCO

_____, Patriotic gore.   PAGO

_____, ed., The shock of recognition.   SHRE

_____, The shores of light.   SHLI

_____, Triple thinkers.   TRTH

_____, The wound and the bow.   WOBO

Wilson, William E., Indiana: a history.   INDA

Wimsatt, William K., Jr. & Cleanth Brooks,
    Literary criticism.   LISH

Winters, Yvor, In defense of reason.   INDR

Woolf, Virginia, Collected essays, v. 1.   COES

_____, Collected essays, v. 3.   COESA

_____, Collected essays, v. 4.   COESB

_____, The common reader.   CORE

Yevtushenko, Yevgeny, Poetry of Yevgeny
Yevtushenko.   POYY

_____, Selected poems.   SELP

Ziff, Larzer, The American 1890's.   AMEI

Ziolkowski, Theodore, Dimensions of the modern
novel.   DIMN